Essential Delphi 2.0 *Fast*
How to Develop Applications in Delphi 2.0

Springer
London
Berlin
Heidelburg
New York
Barcelona
Budapest
Hong Kong
Milan
Paris
Santa Clara
Singapore
Tokyo

John Cowell

Essential Delphi 2.0 *Fast*

How to Develop
Applications in Delphi 2.0

With 216 Figures

 Springer

John Cowell, BSc(Hons), MPhil, PhD
Department of Computer and Information Sciences
De Montfort University
Kents Hill Campus, Hammerwood Gate, Kents Hill
Milton Keynes, MK7 6HP, UK

ISBN 3-540-76026-1 Springer-Verlag Berlin Heidelberg New York

British Library Cataloguing in Publication Data
Cowell, John R.
    Essential Delphi 2.0 fast: how to develop applications in Delphi
    1. Delphi (Computer program language)2. Programming (Electronic computers)
    I.Title
    005.2'62
    ISBN 3540760261

Library of Congress Cataloging-in-Publication Data
Cowell, John, 1957-
    Essential Delphi 2.0 fast: how to develop applications in Delphi / John Cowell
        p.   cm.
    Includes index.
    ISBN 3-540-76026-1 (pbk. : alk. paper)
    1. Delphi (Computer file)   2. Computer software-development.
I. Title.
QA76.76.D47C69   1996
005.265-dc20   96-33758

Microsoft, MS, Visual Basic, Windows are trademarks of Microsoft Corporation
Delphi is a trademark of Borland Corporation

The use of registered names, trademarks etc. in this publication does not imply, even in the
absence of a specific statement, that such names are exempt from the relevant laws and
regulations and therefore free for general use.

The publishers makes no representation, express or implied, with regard to the accuracy of the
information contained in this book and cannot accept any legal responsibility or liability for
any errors or omissions that may be made.

Typeset from disk by T & A Typesetting Services, Rochdale
Printed and bound at the Athenaeum Press Ltd., Gateshead, Tyne and Wear
36 830-5 421 Printed on acid-free paper

Contents

1

Why Use Delphi?

Introduction

Windows has sold several million copies world-wide and is the second best-selling piece of software of all time – after DOS. Windows 95 is breaking all sales records in its first year and is now the standard operating system for PCs. If you are developing software either as a professional programmer, a student or just for fun, it is very probable that you are working in a Windows 95 environment. Delphi is the latest and best way of developing Windows 95 applications, especially for large systems where Visual Basic is not fast enough and the preferred programming language is Pascal. This book runs Delphi version 2 for Windows 95, which is now standard on all new PCs.

Delphi offers a complete development environment for producing professional standard applications. The environment is very intuitive to use and if you already have some programming experience, you can expect to use Delphi confidently after about three weeks' practice and with proficiency after about three months. This is similar to the time taken to learn Visual Basic, and a fraction of the time taken to learn Visual C++. Delphi offers an excellent compromise between the two Microsoft products – Visual C++ and Visual Basic. Most experienced programmers find that they prefer the Delphi environment to those products, and if you are developing Windows software, these are the only alternatives worth considering. Inexperienced programmers who meet Delphi as their first language find it an excellent development environment and are often horrified if they later have to switch to some other language that lacks the features and ease of use of Delphi.

Delphi allows you to develop programs with the same professional feel as the best-selling programs sold for hundreds of pounds. The chances are that whatever you want to do in a Windows 95 environment, Delphi will let you do it.

One annoying characteristic of Delphi for British users is that there are a number of US spellings such as "Dialog" and "Color". In order to avoid confusion I have retained the US spellings in cases like this, otherwise I have kept to British conventions.

Is This Book For You?

This book assumes that you have no prior knowledge of either Delphi or Pascal, the latter being the background programming language for Delphi; however it does assume that you have had some experience of programming in a high-level language. Even if you have already used Pascal, it is worthwhile looking at Chapter 16 (Pascal Primer) if your skills are a bit rusty and you need to refresh them, or if you have used a different Pascal dialect from the Borland variety. This book is also suitable for those at an intermediate level who want to learn how to develop serious, professional applications. It is assumed that you have some experience of using Windows 95 programs such as word processors, spreadsheets and databases.

Many Visual Basic programmers are switching to Delphi, and Chapter 18 is specifically written for Visual Basic programmers who want to make this switch. Visual Basic offers an excellent graphical interface, but it is slow and you need to distribute Dynamic Link Libraries (DLLs) to customers with your applications to enable them to run. Delphi produces executable files that can be distributed without the need for any support environment. If you are a Visual Basic programmer you will find it straightforward to make the switch to Delphi, which has an even better programming environment and compiled programs that run much faster.

If you are a Visual C++ programmer you will be surprised at how easy it is to develop applications in Delphi compared with the Visual C++ environment. Delphi is also object oriented and produces programs that run almost as fast. The executable files tend to be of similar size.

When learning Delphi it is helpful if you already have some programming experience, but all the essential elements of the Delphi Pascal language are covered. If you have used Pascal or 'C' before, you will be able to switch to Delphi without any problems.

Version 2 of Delphi by Borland is a challenge to the highly successful Visual Basic version 4 development environment produced by Microsoft however, although the manuals supplied are fairly comprehensive, they are not error free. The on-line Help is good – the sort of standard that you expect from a major company such as Borland. These facilities are fine if you have a good grasp of Delphi and need to look up a specific point. What the manuals and Help are not very good at, is providing a readable, impartial guide to the language and environment. This book does not cover every minor detail of Delphi in the same way as the manuals, but it does give you a grasp of all the most important features of the language There are many illustrations and examples. The best way to learn Delphi is to try out the examples for yourself.

How to Use This Book

You can either use this book as a guide, starting at the beginning and working through to the end, or just look at individual chapters if you already have some experience of Delphi. How projects are organised and the key features of Delphi are covered in the first part of the book, while more advanced topics such as using databases are covered later. This book is not intended to be a definitive in-depth description of Delphi – if it was it would be about ten times as long and take twenty times as long to read. The philosophy of this book is to cover the key features of Delphi, with many examples and diagrams. Most people find that at first they do not need to learn everything about the language to be able to develop useful programs. If, for example, your first Delphi program does not use databases, you do not need to read the chapter on databases in order to start. The best way to use this book is to read the sections you need and to try the examples. One of the pleasures of Delphi is that it allows you to develop applications fast – you do not even need to read all of this book before you can start!

What Computer You Need to Run Delphi

Computers are never fast enough and rarely have enough disk space or memory, so the faster and more powerful your computer the better. Realistically though, Delphi can be run with quite a modest configuration and still provide reasonable performance.

The minimum configuration for reasonable performance is:

- 80486dx4 or better
- 8 Mb of memory
- 80 Mb of disk space.

Delphi runs successfully on the minimum configuration; however, it does not run fast unless you have a higher specification computer and, if you are serious about developing applications with Delphi, you will need a more powerful computer. There are great improvements in performance when using a Pentium processor with more than 16 Mb of memory.

If you want to run Delphi at the same time as other Windows software, you should have even more memory than this in order to reduce the amount of swapping between disk and memory, which is much slower than referring to memory alone. The minimum amount of disk space is 40 Mb, but a full implementation needs 80 Mb.

What's New in Delphi 2

Delphi 1 was designed to run under Windows 3.1 or 3.11 although it will still run under Windows 95. Delphi 2 has been upgraded for Windows 95 and a number of significant improvements made. This book deals specifically with Delphi 2.

If you are switching from Delphi 1, you will find that the applications that you have developed can be recompiled and linked without problems under the new version, but there are some changes that you should make to ensure that your applications are fully Windows 95 compatible. This section is designed for existing Delphi programmers and covers the most important differences between Delphi 1 and Delphi 2.

New Versions

Delphi 2 is available in three versions:

- Delphi Desktop. This is the base version, and is suitable for most software developers, providing that you are not writing complex database applications.
- Delphi Developer. This is the version which will be used by most professional software developers. It offers some useful enhancements over the Desktop version. A single user, desktop SQL server is provided for building and testing applications. The 32-bit version of ReportSmith is included. The extended Open Tools API allows you to add custom development tools. Additional OCX files are included, such as a spell checker and graph drawing system. The source code for the Visual Component Library is provided. This version is about 50% more expensive than the Desktop version.
- Delphi Client/Server. This version offers all the extra facilities of the Developer version and some extra features. The SQL explorer allows you to browse and modify specific data for Oracle, SyBase, InterBase and Microsoft SQL Servers. The SQL monitor allows you to test, debug and tune database applications. The 32-bit version of the Visual Query Builder is included. Finally an integrated version control system is provided for a team of developers to work together. While this version does offer many enhancements over the Desktop and Developer versions it is about six times the price and therefore only likely to be used in a professional environment where the best possible database development tools possible are required.

All the examples in this book can be done using the Desktop version.

Speed

Many programmers have switched to Delphi from Visual Basic so that their applications will run faster. Delphi 1 programs typically ran 3 times faster than

Visual Basic applications. Borland have this increased this advantage over the Microsoft product with Delphi 2. Programs compiled under Delphi 2 using the 32-bit optimising compiler typically run 3 to 4 times faster than the same 16-bit Delphi 1 code. So just recompiling your existing applications will produce a major benefit even if you are not interested in any other feature of Delphi 2.

Converting from Delphi 1 to Delphi 2.

Converting programs to Delphi 2 is straightforward, but there are a few differences which may cause problems.

- VBX files have been replaced with the 32-bit versions called OCX files. There are many third parties producing VBX files. These are now being converted to OCX files, but it may cause some problems if your VBX supplier is slow in switching to a Windows 95 environment. OCX and OLE files can now be included in applications in the same way that VBX files were included in Delphi 1.
- The four VBX components supplied with Delphi 1 which are no longer available, these are the **TBiSwitch**, **TBiGauge**, **TBiPict** and **TChart**.
- Some Windows 3.1 API functions are different in Windows 95.

You can recompile a Delphi 1 application with Delphi 2. This modifies the resource (RES) file in a way which will not be recognised by Delphi 1. Backward compatibility is not maintained for resource files.

The Visual Component Library

The control palette has changed to include 11 pages of components compared to the 8 pages of version 1, however the change is not as great as might be expected:

- The **Standard** page is unchanged
- The **Additional** page no longer has the **TTabset**, **TNoteBook**, **TTabbedNotebook**, **TOutline** and **THeader** components. These components are specifically for Windows 3.1 and have been placed on a new page called **Win 3.1**, with a further two components, **DBLookupList** and **DBLookupCombo**.
- The **Win 95** page is new and contains a number of specifically designed components for Windows 95. Most of these are direct replacements for the components now on the **Win 3.1** page. For example, the **TPageControl** component is the Windows 95 version of the **TTabbedNoteBook** component. If you are updating an application written under version 1 it would be good to replace the old components with the new ones.
- The **Data Controls** page is the same except that the **TDBLookupList** and **TDBLookupCombo** components have been replaced by the **TDBLookupList-**

Box and **TDBLookupComboBox** components. The new components function in the same way

- The **Dialogs System**, and **Samples** pages are unchanged.
- The **Data Access** page has had an additional two components added, **TSession** and **TUpdateSQL**. The **TReport** component has been deleted.
- The **VBX** page has been replaced with the new **OCX** page.
- The **QReport** page is completely new and provides a way of using the QuickReport facility.

Language and Compiler Changes

Delphi 2 supports strings of virtually unlimited length in addition to strings of up to 255 characters supported by Delphi 1. The compiler directive **$H** determines whether the type **String** represents the old or new string type. A default of **$H+** indicates that the long type is supported. You can of course specify a string of a specific length as before.

The **Variant** data type (widely used in Visual Basic) has been introduced. This data type can change to be either a string, integer or floating point value, depending on what data type it is assigned to.

The new **Currency** data type is a high accuracy fixed point type.

Extensive optimisation has been introduced, there is a detailed description in the **Help** under the heading **Compiler Optimisations**. This does yield speed improvements of 3 or 4 times. Unfortunately most programs take about twice as long to compile. The compiler does give greatly improved error messages and can provide multiple error messages instead of stopping at the first error encountered. To get help on an error, click on the error message and press **F1** to get an explanation of what the error is.

Menu Changes

The menu has been reorganised in a more logical way.

- The **Compile** and **Options** menus have been deleted.
- The **Project**, **Component** and **Database** menus have been added.

In addition numerous other minor changes have been made which are covered later.

The Object Repository

The Object Repository is a means of sharing forms, dialog boxes and data modules. In Delphi 1, it was possible to save forms and dialog boxes as templates.

Data modules could be a part of more than one project, it was simply necessary to refer to the name of the existing data module in the project file. The Object Repository provides a convenient way or organising this re-use.

The repository also allows you to share items such as forms within a project. The Object Repository is reached from the **New** option on the **File** menu. This displays the New Items dialog. If you want to create a new form identical to one already within your project select the page in the dialog with the name of the current project.

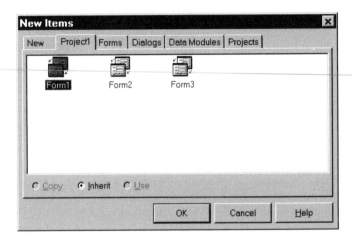

Fig. 1.1 *The Object Repository*

In fig 1.1 the active project is called *Project1* and contains three forms called *Form1*, *Form2* and *Form3*. To create another form identical to one of these forms simply select the form and click on **OK**. A new form is created with all the components and attributes of the existing form.

Database Enhancements

The new 32-bit Borland Database Engine (BDE) is built into version 2, offering improved speed and functionality for use with a wide range of databases including Access, FoxPro, and SQL databases such as Oracle.

Three new data aware controls are provided, **DBLookupListBox**, **DBLookup-ComboBox** and available in all versions of Delphi, while the **DBCtrlGrid** is not available in the Desktop version.

Conventions

There are a few conventions used in this book which make it easier to read:

- All program examples are in *italics*.
- All reserved words such as **begin...end** are in **Bold**.
- All user defined names such as *MyFile* are in *italics*.
- Menu options such as the **Close** option from the **File** menu are in **Bold.**

2

Running Delphi

Introduction

In this section you will learn about:

- Running Delphi.
- The interactive tutors.
- The main features of the Delphi development environment.

Starting Delphi

When you install Delphi it creates a new folder called Delphi. In order to run Delphi:

- Click on **Start** from the Windows 95 taskbar.
- Select the **Programs** icon from the first menu.
- Click on **Borland Delphi 2.0** from the second menu.
- Finally click on **Delphi 2.0** in the third menu.

This is shown in fig. 2.1.

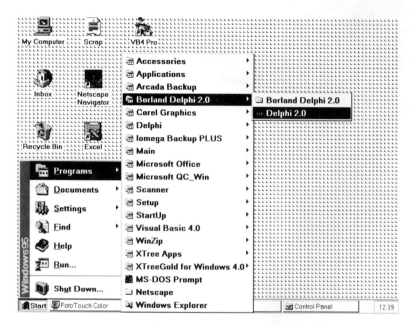

Fig. 2.1   *Launching Delphi*

When the Delphi design screen is first displayed as shown in fig. 2.2, it looks very confusing at first, but each part of it has a well-defined role.

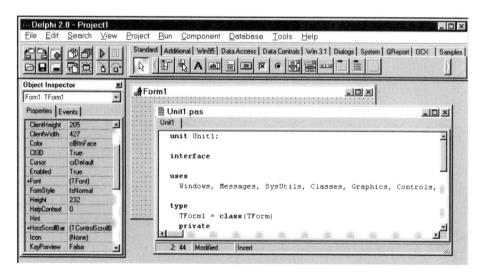

Fig. 2.2   *The Delphi design screen*

Before you look in detail at each of these components it is worthwhile using the three interactive tutors which are supplied as a part of **Help**. These are very basic but do provide a quick introduction. To run the interactive tutors click on **Help Topics** on the **Help** menu and search for *Interactive Tutors* in the index. The tutors are:

- Introducing Delphi.
- Creating a simple application.
- Database Applications.

At this stage just try the first two tutors – they should each take about fifteen to twenty minutes. If you do try to run the Database Applications tutor you will find that it runs very slowly unless you have a lot of memory (12 Mb or more). This tutor is so slow that it is virtually unusable unless you have a fast computer with a lot of memory.

The Delphi Programming Environment

There are five visible parts to the Delphi programming environment on the Delphi design screen:

- The Form.
- The Component Palette.
- The Object Inspector.
- The Code Editor.
- The SpeedBar.

The Form

The design form (fig. 2.3) is the focal part of the design screen.

This has the default heading of *Form1*. If you create a second form it has the default name of *Form2* and so on. The naming sequence is logical but not imaginative. If you want to change it, you can.

The grid dots are used to align controls on a form. When you insert a control such as a button or list, it "snaps" to the nearest grid point. You can alter the spacing of the grid points or disable the grid altogether. Each type of control has a set of configurable properties associated with it.

This form has all the usual features of a window. The hot spots are used for re-sizing the form. When the mouse pointer is on a hot spot, a double-ended arrow is shown. By pressing the left mouse button and dragging, the form border can be moved to shrink or enlarge the form. When the minimise button is pressed, the window disappears and a new button appears on the taskbar. You can return to this window by clicking on this taskbar button as shown in fig. 2.4. Windows 95 does allow you to reposition the taskbar to any edge of your screen just by dragging, but the usual place is along the bottom of the screen.

Title bar   Minimise/maximise Close window

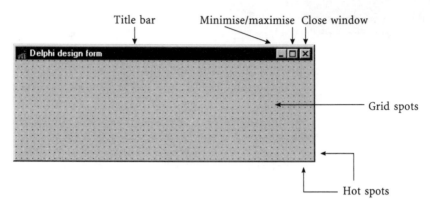

Grid spots

Hot spots

Fig. 2.3   *The design form*

Fig. 2.4   *The Windows 95 taskbar*

Every Delphi program has at least one form which is used to design the user interface that you want for your program. The Component Palette provides the tools to add buttons, text boxes, captions, combo boxes and all the other standard Windows elements that make up the user interface. All of these elements are called components.

Another way of maximising or minimising a form is to click on the right mouse button while the mouse cursor is over the appropriate button on the taskbar and to select one of the options as shown in fig. 2.5.

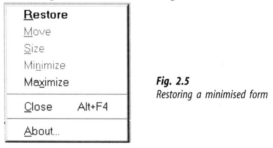

Fig. 2.5
Restoring a minimised form

When a form is maximised, it occupies the entire screen.

The Component Palette

Components (these are called controls in Visual Basic) are the key elements of a Windows application. They include all the expected features of the user interface of an application, such as buttons, combo boxes and text boxes.

In order to place a component on a form, click on the component key and then click on the form. The component appears in the position that you click.

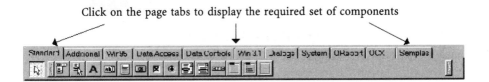

Click on the page tabs to display the required set of components

Fig. 2.6 *The Standard Component Palette*

Delphi offers a wide range of components which are logically grouped in pages. You can switch between pages by clicking on one of the page tabs. The most frequently used components are on the Standard page, which is shown in fig. 2.6.

You can create your own components or install Visual Basic OCX controls.

All of the standard components and the most important components on the other pages are described later.

The Object Inspector

You can select a component in Delphi by clicking on it. In the form shown, a **TMemo** component called *Memo1* is selected. This is indicated by the eight sizing handles on the component. You can change the size of the component by clicking on one of the handles and then dragging, keeping the left mouse button pressed (fig. 2.7). You can also drag a selected component by clicking on it, anywhere apart from the sizing handles, and dragging (keeping the left mouse button pressed).

Every component has a range of properties which control how it behaves and looks. When you create a new component it is given a default set of properties which you can both view and change. When a component has been selected, its properties are displayed in the Object Inspector.

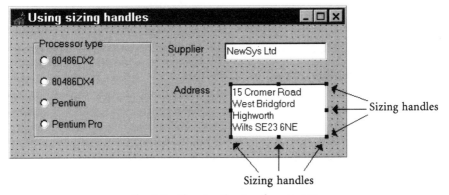

Fig. 2.7 *Changing the size of components*

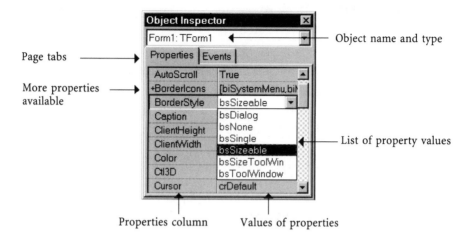

Fig. 2.8   *The Object Inspector*

The Object Inspector has two columns, the left giving the name of the property and the right column giving the value of that property. If you want to change a property at design time, click on that property. Some properties, such as the **Caption** property, have to be typed, while others can be selected from a list. This second group of properties have a small downward arrow on the far right of the property value column as shown for the **BorderStyle** property in fig. 2.8. When you click on this, the available values for that property are shown.

Some properties listed are in fact objects rather than simple properties, for example, the **Font** object has properties of **Color, Size** and **Style**. To change the **Font** you must change one of these properties. You can spot the objects from the simple properties by looking for the small "+" sign on the far left of the property name. If you click on the "+" the properties of the object are displayed.

If you want to keep the Object Inspector visible at all times, click the right button on the mouse and choose the **StayOn Top** option from the SpeedMenu.

At the top of the Object Inspector there are two page tabs. The one shown first is the Properties page; the other is the Events page. You can switch between them by clicking on the page tab.

The Events page lists all the events that may be associated with the component, for example, a button has a click event.

The Code Editor

The code editor is a powerful editor which allows you to edit all of the Pascal code in the application.

When a new project is started, Delphi creates a unit for the source code. Every time you create a new form, a new unit is created. By default the first unit is called

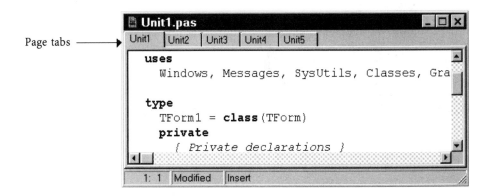

Fig. 2.9 *The code editor*

unit1.pas, the second unit2.pas. If you want to view the source code for a unit, click on the page tab for that unit.

The SpeedBar

The SpeedBar (fig. 2.10) contains a short-cut way of using some of the most common features available in the Delphi menu bar. If you forget what the icons mean, simply hold the mouse over the icon for a second and a useful prompt is displayed.

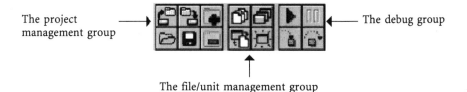

The file/unit management group

Fig. 2.10 *The SpeedBar*

The SpeedBar can be configured to include any of the items available via the menu. The default has three groups of buttons for dealing with project management, file and unit management, and debugging The menu bar and the SpeedBar are dealt with later. At first it is best to use the menu before trying to use short-cuts.

3

The Disappearing Memo

Introduction

At this point the Delphi development environment should look more familiar, but Delphi is a large system and the best way to become familiar with it is to develop an application. In this chapter you are going to produce a program that has a single form with a text box which disappears when a button is clicked and reappears when it is clicked again. For Delphi this is straightforward; it would take a proficient programmer a few minutes, compared with hours for any common third generation programming language such as Turbo Pascal or C.

If you are not familiar with Pascal or need to refresh your skills, you should look at Chapter 16, or at least refer to it in order to follow the examples from here onwards.

In this chapter you will learn about:

- Event driven software.
- Adding components to forms.
- Changing component properties.
- Compiling and linking programs.
- Running programs.

Event Driven Software

If you have programmed before in languages such as Pascal or C, you need to think in a different way to program in Delphi. When a Windows program runs, the user is usually presented with a screen comprising a form with a number of controls, such as buttons, lists, or edit boxes. The user decides what happens next by perhaps clicking on a button or selecting a list item or inputting text.

Everything the user does is viewed by the application as an event, and the programmer who writes the application needs to make sure that every event that occurs is dealt with. This is called event driven software.

In Delphi every event has both a name and an event procedure associated with it which makes a response to that event. For example if you click on a button, an **OnClick** event occurs. You need to write some Pascal code to take the appropriate action. Delphi produces template event procedures for events that you want to respond to and transfers program control to them. You have to write the code to control what happens in response to the event.

Delphi makes sure that the program control goes to the appropriate event handler when that event happens, without the need to write complex interrupt driven software.

Creating the User Interface

The best way to learn a new programming environment is to use it. The first Delphi application you are going to look at has a single form with two components, a **TButton** and a **TMemo** component. When the button is clicked the **TMemo** component disappears; when it is clicked again the **TMemo** component reappears (fig. 3.1)

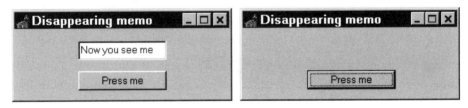

Fig. 3.1 *Using the **Visible** property of the text box*

The first stage is to create the form and the associated unit code, which contains all the event handlers for the form. When you run Delphi this is done automatically for you.

If you have been experimenting with Delphi and have already added components to the form or written any supporting Pascal code, you need to start a new application. Click on the **New application** option from the **File** menu. This asks you where you want to save your existing application and then start a new application.

Fig. 3.2
*The **TMemo** component*

To add the **TMemo** component (fig. 3.2), click on the **TMemo** component button. When you move the cursor over the memo button, a help message is displayed, so it should be easy to display. Make sure that you have the Standard page selected (fig. 3.3).

Fig. 3.3   *The Standard page on the Component Palette*

- Click on the form in the position that you want the memo box to go. Do not worry if it is in the wrong position or is the wrong size, this can be changed later.
- Click on the **TButton** component (fig. 3.4) and click again on the form where you want to position it.

Fig. 3.4
The **TButton** *component*

- Change the size of the components by first clicking on a component to select it and then dragging the sizing handles.
- Move the components to the chosen position by clicking the left mouse button on the component and dragging it.

Your application should now look something like that shown in fig. 3.5.

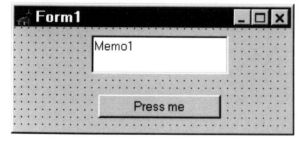

Fig. 3.5
The design form so far

Finding Windows

One of the most frustrating things about working in a new environment that has many windows is that it is not always easy to find the window you want.

- If you want to find a form select the **Forms** option from the **View** menu.
- If you want to find the supporting code files, called units, select the **Units** option from the **View** menu.

The **View** menu also provides an easy way of finding all the windows in the Delphi environment.

Changing Component Properties

The next stage is to change the title of the form from the default *Form1 to Disappearing memo*. First select the form by clicking anywhere on it. The Object Inspector will automatically change to display the properties and events associated with the form.

Make sure that the **Properties** page of the Object Inspector and not the **Event** page is displayed. If necessary, click on the page tab marked Properties at the top of the Object Inspector.

The property of the form that determines the title is the **Caption**. Click on the column on the right of the **Caption** property which contains the text *Form1*. Delete it by using the delete or backspace key and type the new title *Disappearing memo component*. As you type, you will see it appear at the top of the form.

Note that there is also a **Name** property called *Form1*. This is used in your program to refer to this component. It is a common error to change this property instead of the **Caption** property.

To change the text on the button from *Button1* to *Press Me* the same operation has to be carried out. Click on the button to select it and change the **Caption** property from *Button1* to *Press Me*. If you find that there is insufficient space for the text to fit onto the button, just stretch the button using the sizing handles. This button also has a **Name** property with a value of *Button1*.

Changing the text displayed in the **TMemo** component is a little more difficult. The text is stored in the **Lines** property (fig. 3.6) of the component. Select the **TMemo** component and find that property. There are three dots on the right of this property which indicate that a sub menu is available.

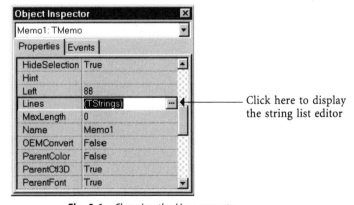

Fig. 3.6 *Changing the Lines property*

Click on the dots and the string list editor is displayed (fig. 3.7).

Fig. 3.7
The strings list editor

Type the text that you want to be displayed – replacing the default text *Memo1* with *Now you see me*. Click on **OK** when you have done this.

If you want to use this text again, you can save it in a file by pressing the right mouse button over the string list editor and selecting the **Save** option. You are prompted for a text file to save this text. Specify the file name and click on **OK**. Click **OK** again to leave the string list editor.

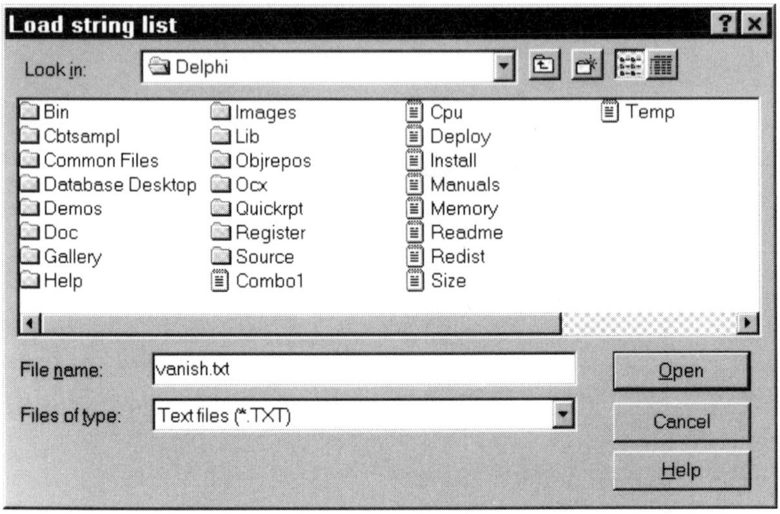

Fig. 3.8 *Saving text using the string list editor*

If you had already prepared some text in another file, you could have used that by pressing the right mouse button while over the string list editor and selecting the **Load** option.

Running the Program

In order to run the program it must be compiled and linked. If you select the **Run** option from **Run** on the main menu, the program is compiled, linked and run.

If you run this program you see that the form you have created is displayed. The form can be re-sized and minimised and maximised, but nothing happens when you click on the button. To get the memo box to appear and disappear you need to write some Pascal code.

Your program can be stopped in the usual way by double clicking on the top left corner of the form.

Writing the Pascal Code

A property of memo boxes is **Visible**. When this is set to true the memo is displayed; when it is false it disappears. The Pascal code that you need to write sets the **Visible** property to false if it is true (making it disappear) and to true if it is false (making it appear).

Every component has a set of events that it deals with, for example, a button can deal with a click or double click event. You need to write some Pascal that changes the **Visible** property of the memo box in response to a click event occurring.

Delphi creates template procedures for event handlers. To go to this template, select the button and choose the Events page of the Object Inspector.

Double click on the **OnClick** event as shown in fig. 3.9; the template procedure for the click event for this button is displayed in the code editor window.

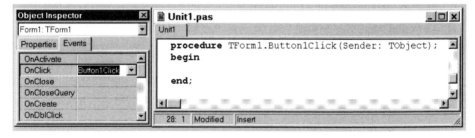

Fig. 3.9 *The OnClick event handler*

Button1Click is the name of the event procedure for the button called *Button1*. The only code that you need to add is between the **begin** and **end** pair. You look at the other features of these procedures later. The code needed is:

> *if memo1.Visible = true*
> **then**
>   *memo1.Visible := false*
> **else**
>   *memo1.Visible := true;*

The **Visible** property of the memo whose name is *memo1* is referred to as *memo1*.**Visible**. This can be assigned the values of either true or false.

Not all properties can be changed at run-time, but those that can are referred to in the same way, by specifying the component name, a period and then the component property.

When additional event handlers or components are added, Delphi automatically makes changes to the Pascal, as we see later. However, it is not necessary to know about this to create simple working applications. If you compile and link the program now, you see that it performs as intended.

4

How Projects are Organised

Introduction

When you are creating an application in Delphi, all the necessary files are grouped together in a project, which is usually stored in its own folder. The first stage in developing an application is to create a new project. In this section you will learn about:

- Project elements.
- Creating Forms.
- Creating and saving modules.
- Using the Project Manager.
- Using the search facility in **Help**.

File Types in Delphi Project

Since projects are normally stored in their own folder you should create a new folder for your application before starting to develop the application in Delphi. New folders can be created by using either the Windows Explorer or other packages such as XTreeWin.

Some files are generated at design time, while others are produced when the project is compiled and linked.

Design-time Project Files

The main design-time resource files are:

- A Project (DPR) file. This file lists details of all the form and unit files in the project. It is a Pascal file despite its extension.
- Unit Source (PAS) files. One source file is created for every form created in the project.
- Graphical form (DFM) files. One file is created for every PAS file in the project and contains design information on that file.
- Project options (OPT) file. This is a text file containing details of the project options. There is only one such file per project.

Compiler Generated Files

The compiler generated files are:

- Executable (EXE) file. This is the completed runnable application.
- Unit object code (DCU) file. This is an object file created for every PAS file. You do not need to save these files for your EXE file to run.
- Dynamic link library (DLL) file. A dynamic link library file can be created instead of an EXE file.

Project Files

There is only one DPR or project file per project. It is the main program file and is essential if all the other components of the project are to be compiled into an executable program. Delphi creates and changes this file as you create and delete new source for the project and so, although it is a text file, it should never be necessary to change it manually.

Unit Source Files and Graphical Form Files

You can create as many PAS files as you wish for your project; however, when you create a new application only a single PAS file is created. Each contains Pascal source code. A file may form a part of one or more projects.

PAS files are often connected with DFM files, which contain a graphical description of a form. There is one DFM file for each form. While there is always a PAS file associated with a DFM file, PAS files do not necessarily need a DFM file.

Files You Need to Edit

Although there seems to be a complex set of different files in a Delphi project, most are maintained by Delphi itself; in fact, the only files that you ever need to edit and change manually are the unit source or PAS files.

The Project Manager

Delphi has a useful tool for managing projects which can open, save, delete or amend all the files in a project. It cannot be used to create a new project, but this is not needed since when you run Delphi, it automatically opens a default project.

To use the **Project Manager,** select the **Project Manager** option from the **View** menu.

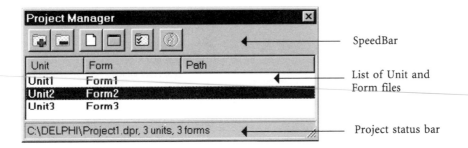

Fig. 4.1 *The Project Manager*

The project status bar in fig. 4.1 indicates the location of the project (DPR) file and the number of units and forms in the projects, while the project file list gives the names of all forms and units in the project. This information is obtained from the projects file, which is updated automatically when the files making up the project are changed. Serious problems can be caused if you create files outside of Delphi, since you need to change the DPR file manually, which is not recommended.

The SpeedBar

The project status bar and the lists of form and unit files are for information only, while the SpeedBar allows you to change and view the files in the project.

SpeedBar Button	Action
Add	Adds a new file to the project.
Remove	Removes a file from the project (but does not delete it).
View Unit	Displays the selected unit.
View Form	Displays the selected form.
Project Options	Displays the Project Options dialog box.
Update	Updates the Project Manager information displayed by referring to the DPR file. This is not needed unless you have manually changed the DPR file.

The Program Manager SpeedMenu

An alternative way of carrying out these functions is to use the Program Manager SpeedMenu (fig. 4.2), which you call up by pressing the right mouse button from anywhere within the Project Manager.

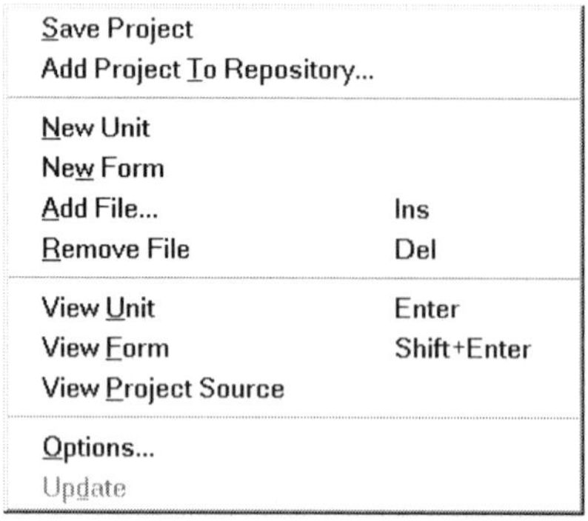

```
Save Project
Add Project To Repository...

New Unit
New Form
Add File...              Ins
Remove File             Del

View Unit               Enter
View Form               Shift+Enter
View Project Source

Options...
Update
```

Fig. 4.2
The Program Manager SpeedMenu

In addition, the SpeedMenu allows you to save a project at any time, and also to save it as a template. This option is useful if you want to use the current project as the basis for another project. When you start another project, you can specify this template and have access to all forms and files of the original project.

The Project Options dialog, shown in fig. 4.3, can be displayed by selecting **Options** from this SpeedMenu. This can be used to control all aspects of the project.

The Project Options Dialog

In addition to being called from the **Options** choice in the SpeedMenu, the Project Options dialog box can be invoked two other ways:

- Select **Options** from the main **Project** menu.
- Select the **Options** SpeedMenu from the Program Manager.

There are five pages in the Projects Option Dialog:

- Forms.
- Application.
- Compiler.
- Linker.
- Directories/Conditionals.

The Forms Option

This option, shown in fig. 4.3, allows you to change the form that is used as the main form of the project. By default the main form is the first one you create and,

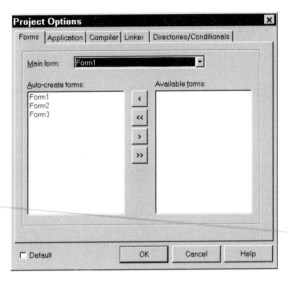

Fig. 4.3   *The Forms page from the Projects Options dialog*

unless you specify otherwise in your application, it is loaded into memory first. The main form is automatically created at run-time.

The Application Options

This option, shown in fig. 4.4, specifies the title and the name of the help file for your application. You can also specify an icon that can be used to run your program from Windows.

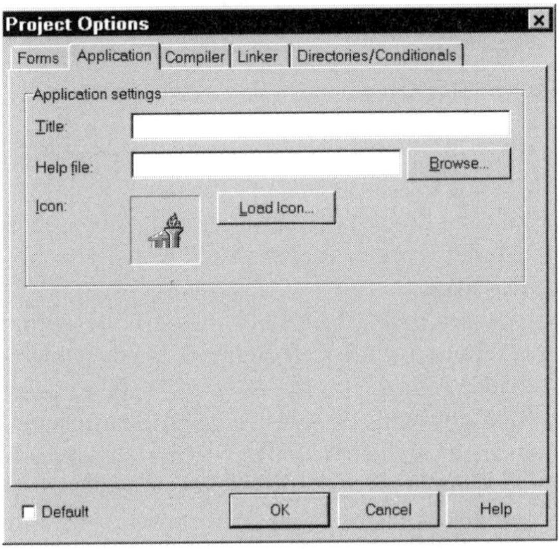

Fig. 4.4   *The Applications page from the Project Options dialog*

Browsers are available to help you find the help file and icon that you want to use.

The Compiler Options

This option, shown in fig. 4.5, changes the way in which the compiler performs. If you change any of the default settings, only the current project is affected unless you click on the *Default* check box, which is located in the bottom left corner of the dialog box.

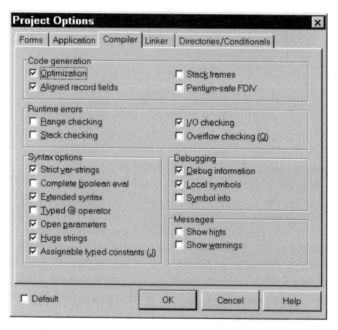

Fig. 4.5   *The Compiler page from the Project Options dialog*

The Borland manuals are not very helpful in saying what each of these options are – you are simply asked to look at the on-line help. The information, when you do locate it, is helpful. The best way is to select **Help** Topic from the **Help** menu and then choose the **Index** option, shown in fig. 4.6.

Search for **Compiler page**.

The options that you are most likely to change are for enabling and disabling the run-time errors. When you are debugging it is advisable to turn on all the run-time error checking, in order to get as much help as possible from Delphi should your application go wrong. It is also a good idea to have all the debugging options switched on since this helps you to use the debugger fully when testing and fixing your applications.

When you have completed testing your applications, you should switch off all the debugging and run-time options. This will make your application run faster as well as reducing its size.

Fig. 4.6 *The Topic Search option from the Help menu*

It is unlikely that you will want to change the syntax options unless you are used to a different compiler that uses these language features.

The Linker Options

When the source files of your application have been compiled, they need to be linked into an executable program. This option, shown in fig. 4.7, controls the performance of the linker.

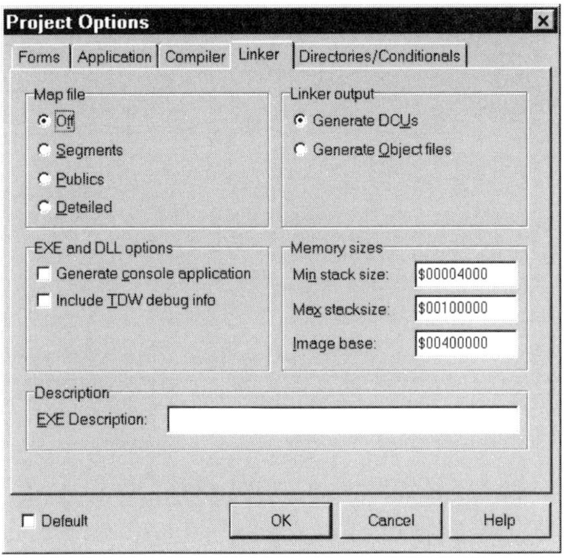

Fig. 4.7 *The Linker page from the Project Options dialog*

By default Delphi does not produce a map file, which contains information about the executable file created when linking, such as the addresses of all the source files in the application; however, Delphi has powerful debugging facilities which means that it is rarely necessary to refer to the map file when a problem occurs.

One of the elements that you may wish to change is the stack size. Delphi saves all local variables on the stack and uses it to pass information between procedures. If you have a lot of local data you may need to increase the stack size. Alternatively, if you have a small application, you can reduce the stack size to save memory.

The Directories/Conditional Options

This is used to specify the directory where the compiled units and the executable program are placed, as shown in fig. 4.8. If this is not specified, the same directory as the project file is used.

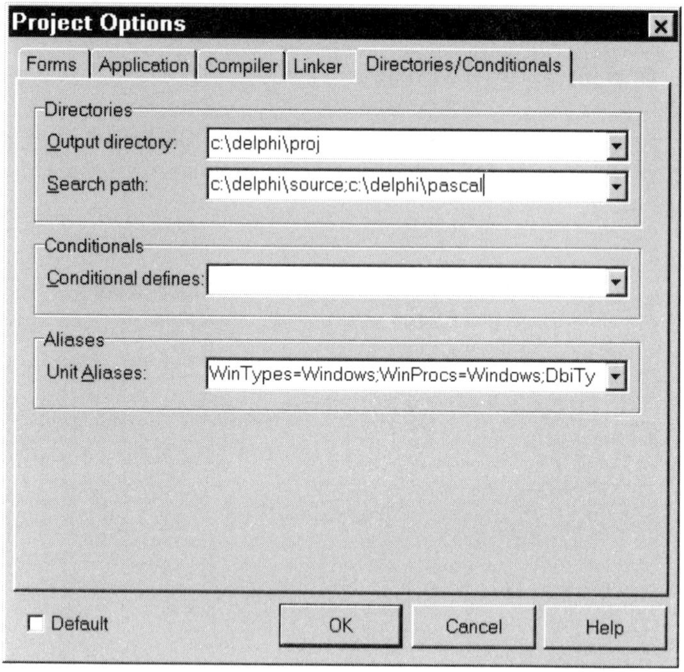

Fig. 4.8   *The Directories/Conditionals page from the Project Options dialog*

The search box is used to specify a list of path names, separated by a semicolon where Delphi looks for the source files when building the application. Delphi only looks along this specified path after looking in the directory where the project file is stored and in the Delphi library directory (...\DELPHI\LIB).

5

The Standard Component Palette

Introduction

The Component Palette has virtually all the components that you are likely to use, but if necessary you can add your own. There are eleven pages in the Component Palette. The most frequently used ones are in the standard palette which is shown by clicking on the Standard page tab of the Component Palette. In this chapter you will learn about the following components on the Standard page:

- TLabel
- TEdit
- TMemo
- TButton
- TCheckBox
- TRadioButton

- TListBox
- TComboBox
- TScrollBar
- TGroupBox
- TRadioGroup

The components on the other pages of the Component Palette are covered in Chapter 15.

The TLabel Component

The **TLabel** component (fig. 5.1) is used to display text that the user cannot change.

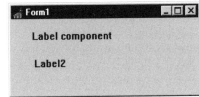

*Fig. 5.1   The **TLabel** component*

The text that is displayed is stored in the **Caption** property of the component.

The **TLabel** component automatically re-sizes to fit the size of the text if the **AutoSize** property is set to true (this is the default). Text can also be aligned to the left, right, or centre by using the **Alignment** property. A useful property of labels is that you can ensure that other components are not obscured by setting the **Transparent** property to true. The first label to be created is called *Label1*, the second is *Label2*, and so on.

The TEdit Component

The **TEdit** component (fig. 5.2) is used to display or read a single line of text.

Fig. 5.2 *The **TEdit** component*

The text that is displayed is stored in the **Text** property.

The font of the text shown can be changed by using the **Font** property. A useful property of **TEdit** components is **Modified**, which is set to true if the contents of the component are changed. The first **TEdit** component is called *Edit1*.

One important property of **TEdit** components is that you can prevent text being displayed on the screen as it is typed if, for example, you are typing a password. This is done by setting the **PassWordChar** property of the component to a single letter, which is echoed every time any printable key is pressed.

The TMemo Component

The **TMemo** component (fig. 5.3) is used to display or read many lines of text – up to a maximum of 255K.

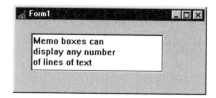

Fig. 5.3 *The **TMemo** component*

The **Lines** property is a string list which contains the text in the memo. In common with the **TLabel** and **TEdit** components, the font and alignment are controlled by the **Font** and **Alignment** properties. The first **TMemo** component is called *Memo1*.

The TButton Component

Buttons are used to initiate some action.

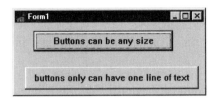

Fig. 5.4 *The **TButton** component*

The two principal events are the **OnClick** and **OnDblClick** events. The first **TButton** component (see fig. 5.4) is called *Button1*. The text on the button is stored in the **Caption** property.

The TCheckBox Component

The **TCheckBox** component (fig. 5.5) is used to indicate if an option is true or false.

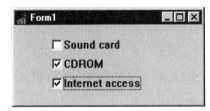

Fig. 5.5 *The **TCheckBox** component*

If the check box is true the box on the left of the component is crossed. The **Checked** property indicates if the check box is checked or not. Sometimes, it is useful to make a check box unavailable to the user, and this is done by setting the **Enabled** property to false. Another useful property of check boxes is to place the check box on either the right or left of its text. This is the **Alignment** property.

The TRadioButton Component

The **TRadioButton** (fig. 5.6) is similar to the **TCheckBox** component in that it is used to indicate a true or false option. The difference is that radio buttons are usually grouped together in either a **TPanel, TGroupBox,** or **TScrollBox** compo-nent. If this is the case, only one of the group of **TRadioButtons** components can be set to true.

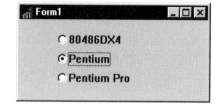

Fig. 5.6 *The* **TRadioButton** *component*

In common with check boxes, radio buttons can be made unavailable by using the **Enabled** property, and the **Alignment** property used to place the button on the right or left of the text.

The TListBox Component

The **TListBox** component (fig. 5.7) displays a scrollable list that the user can select but cannot modify. The only way in which items can be entered into the list is by writing some Pascal code.

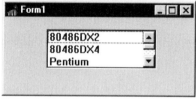

Fig. 5.7 *The* **TListBox** *component*

The text displayed in a list box is a string list specified by the **Items** property. You can display items alphabetically by setting the **Sorted** property to true.

The TComboBox Component

TComboBox components (fig. 5.8) are similar to **TListBox** components except that users can either select an item from a pre-defined list or type their own text.

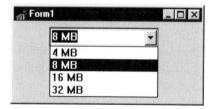

Fig. 5.8 *The* **TComboBox** *component*

The **Items** property contains the text of the list in a string list.

The TScrollBar Component

The **TScrollBar** (fig. 5.9) has a range of uses. The commonest is to indicate which part of a screen is visible by clicking on the arrows at either end of a vertical or horizontal scroll bar; this is used in standard Windows applications such as word processors.

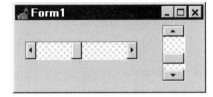

Fig. 5.9 *The TScrollBar component*

Scroll bars can also be used to indicate the level of a quantity such as screen brightness or temperature, without the user having to type text.

The **OnScroll** event is used to deal with a change in the position of the scroll. The minimum and maximum values when the scroll bar is at either extremes of its position are given by the **Min** and **Max** properties of the component.

The TGroupBox Component

This component is used to group other components, such as radio buttons, so that they can be treated as a single group.

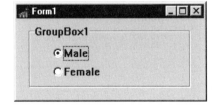

Fig. 5.10 *The TGroupBox component*

The **TGroupBox** component (fig. 5.10) places a box around the grouped components. If you want to box a collection of components without putting them in a group, use the **TBevel** component. When there are a number of radio buttons in a group box, Delphi ensures that only one of the radio buttons can be set.

The TRadioGroup Component

Since radio buttons are virtually always grouped together in a **TGroupBox** component, the **TRadioGroup** component (fig. 5.11) provides a convenient way of creating a set of radio buttons in a group box, rather than using a **TGroupBox** component followed by several **TRadioButton** components. Functionally the two are the same.

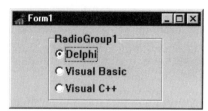

Fig. 5.11   *The **TRadioGroup** component*

To use the **TRadioGroup** component, first select the component and then choose the **Items** property in the Object Inspector, clicking on the three dots on the right of the property. The string list editor is displayed and you are prompted for the text for the first radio button. For each line of text entered a new button is created, until the **OK** button is clicked.

Using the Components

This chapter has looked at some of the most commonly used components, but the best way to learn about the components is to use them. The next chapter looks at writing the user interface side of an application.

6

Computer Buyers Survey

Introduction

We have looked at the key elements of Delphi's user interface. You have seen how projects are created and organised, and also most of the standard components. In this chapter you will learn how to design a substantial form using the ideas that have been introduced so far.

The Completed Form

The form that you are going to create is an enquiry form for computer buyers. The completed form, with some details already entered, is shown in fig. 6.1.

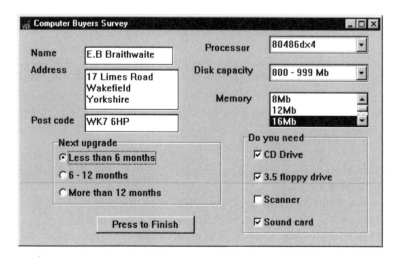

Fig. 6.1 *The completed form*

Using the Grid to Align Components

If the components in a form do not line up with each other, the form does not look professional. Delphi provides a grid to help you improve the look of your forms. The top and left of all components are always aligned to the grid that covers the form. You need to make sure that this option is turned on. Select the **Options** option from the **Tools** menu to display the **Preferences** box as shown in fig. 6.2.

Fig. 6.2   *Using the grid to align components*

Click on the **Display grid** check box option to make the grid visible and also the **Snap to grid** check box so that the component is inserted at the nearest grid point. A default grid size of 8 seems to be fine for most forms.

Creating the Form

- The first stage is to create a new project. Select the **New Application** option from the **File** menu.
- Go to the Properties page of the Object Inspector and change the **Caption** property of the form to *Computer Buyers Survey*.
- Click on the **TLabel** component in the standard palette and click on the design form in the approximate position where you want the name label to go.
- Change the **Caption** property of the **TLabel** component to *Name*.

- Repeat this for the *Address, Post code, Processor Disk capacity* and *Memory* labels. Do not worry at this stage if a component is not in exactly the right position or if it is not the correct size.
- Click on the **TEdit** component and put a **TEdit** component adjacent to the *Name* label.
- The box for entering the *Post code* is also a **TEdit** component and should be drawn at this stage.
- There is a **TMemo** component adjacent to the *Address* label. Click on the **TMemo** component and insert it in this position.

A memo box is needed since an edit box can only be one line long. The other components used are two combo boxes adjacent to the *Processor* and *Disk capacity* labels. If you cannot remember which component is which on the palette, a pop-up help appears if you place the mouse cursor on a component for more than a second.

- Place combo boxes adjacent to the *Processor* and *Disk capacity* labels.
- Place a list box adjacent to the memory box.

Before creating the group of radio buttons and check boxes, two group boxes must be created. The group box must be made first if the components it surrounds are to be treated as a single group.

- Place the radio buttons in turn in the left group box, changing the **Caption** properties of each to display the correct text.
- Place the check boxes in the right group box, again changing the **Caption** properties of each.
- Finally, place a button on the form.

A list of possible processors and disk capacities needs to be entered into the two combo boxes, while the available memory sizes are entered into a list box. Each combo and list box contains some default text – the same as the component name. To set the text in the combo and list boxes, click on the **Items** property and set the text in the string list editor.

Entering List and Combo Box Data

The name, address and post code are all typed by the user. The check boxes and radio boxes are also checked at run-time, but you need to supply a list of options for the list and combo boxes. The list box has a **Items** property which is of type **TString**. If you select this component and click on the three dots on the right of this property in the Object Inspector, the string list editor is displayed as shown in fig. 6.3.

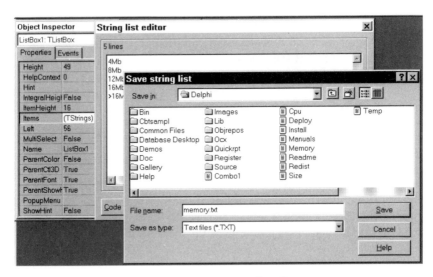

Fig. 6.3   *Using the string list editor*

- Type the text that you want to be displayed in the list box. In this case it is a list of possible sizes of memory that you might find on a PC.
- If you want to save this text in a file, click the right mouse button over the string list editor and select the *Save* option. This displays the Save string list dialog box. Specify the name and place where you want the file containing your text to be saved. In this case use *memory.txt*, and then click on **Save**.
- You do not have to save the text in a file if you do not want to use it in a later application; simply click on **OK** in the string list editor.

Now that all of the components are on the form, you can modify them by selecting a component and using the sizing handles or by dragging the component to a new position.

A quick way of building and running the application is to choose **Run** from the **Run** menu. This builds your application if it has changed since the last time is was run, and then runs it. If an error is found, Delphi pauses at the line of code where the error is and gives you the chance to correct it. You then have to try building and running the application again.

When you build and run the application successfully, you will see the list of memory sizes (fig. 6.4) in the list box.

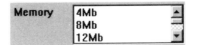

Fig. 6.4
The memory size list box

Not all of the possible options can be displayed in the space available, but there is a vertical scroll bar on the right of the list (this is the default) which allows you to see all of the options and to choose one of them.

The list of items is specified in the same way for the two combo boxes. A section of the screen displaying these lists at run-time is shown in fig. 6.5.

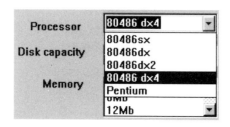 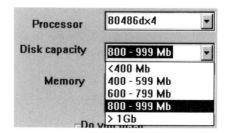

Fig. 6.5 *Using combo boxes*

Run-time Properties

The properties that you have seen so far have been available both at design-time and at run-time, but some properties are only available at run-time.

When you run this program, you do not want to see the text *combobox1* in the first edit box. To change this, the **ItemIndex** property is used. This is a run-time property that cannot be changed at design-time. If **ItemIndex** is set to minus 1, the combo box is initially blank. If it is set to 0, the first entry of the **Items** property is displayed as the default. A value of 1 gives the second value as the default, and so on. The best place for this text is in the form creation event handler.

Double click on the form to go to the event handler for the form creation event. This is executed when the program is run and the form is displayed. Delphi creates the template procedure for you and ensures that this procedure is executed when the program is run – you need to add the two lines between the **begin** and **end** statements.

```
procedure TForm1.FormCreate(Sender: TObject);
begin
    combobox1.ItemIndex := -1;
    combobox2.ItemIndex := 3;
end;
```

Aligning Components

It can be quite difficult to ensure that all components are aligned correctly. Fortunately Delphi provides two ways of aligning components. The first technique is to use the alignment palette:

- Select the components that you want to align.
- Choose the **Alignment Palette** option from the **View** menu. This displays the alignment palette, as shown in fig. 6.6:

Fig. 6.6
Aligning components using the
Alignment Palette

These buttons offer a comprehensive set of controls for aligning components. Where the edges of a set of selected components are to be aligned, this is done using the first component selected as the base.

Icon	Function
	Aligns components to the left edge of the first component selected.
	Aligns the centres of the selected components.
	Aligns components to the centre of the form along a horizontal line.
	Ensures that components are equally spaced horizontally.
	Aligns the right edge of components.
	Aligns the top edge of components.
	Moves the selected components vertically until their centres are aligned with the first component selected.
	Aligns components to the centre of the form along a vertical line.
	Ensures that components are equally spaced vertically.
	Aligns the bottom edge of components.

If you are unsure of what an option does, move the mouse cursor over the palette and you will see a useful help message displayed

The second technique is to use the alignment dialog box:

- Select the components that you want to align.
- Choose the **Align** option from the **Edit** menu.

If, for example, you want the left sides and tops of the selected components to be aligned, choose the options shown in fig. 6.7; note that only one horizontal and one vertical option can be selected, since to select more than one is likely to be contradictory.

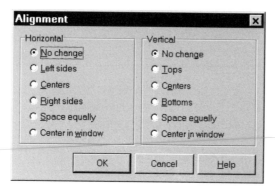

Fig. 6.7   *Aligning components using the* **Align** *option from the* **Edit** *menu*

In both methods, the first component is used as a basis for the alignment of the other components.

The form at this stage is shown in fig. 6.8.

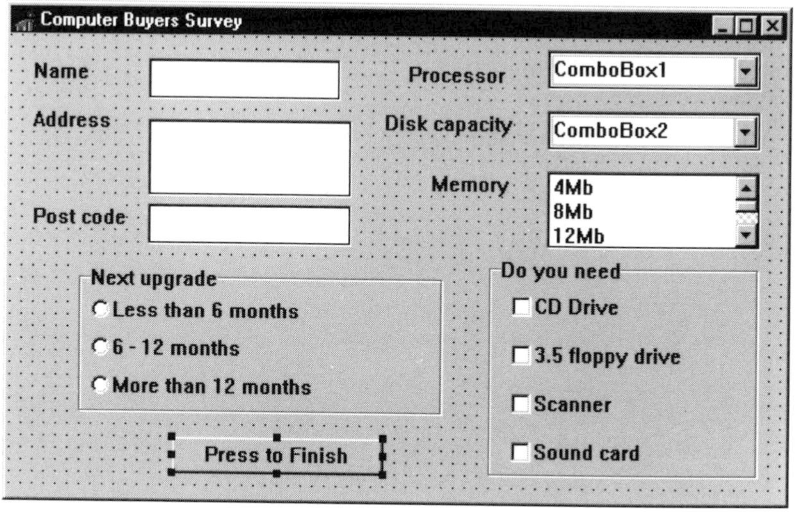

Fig. 6.8   *The completed design screen*

Unit Changes

When you add a new component to a form, Delphi automatically declares that component in the associated unit. Each declaration consists of a name of the component followed by a type (fig. 6.9).

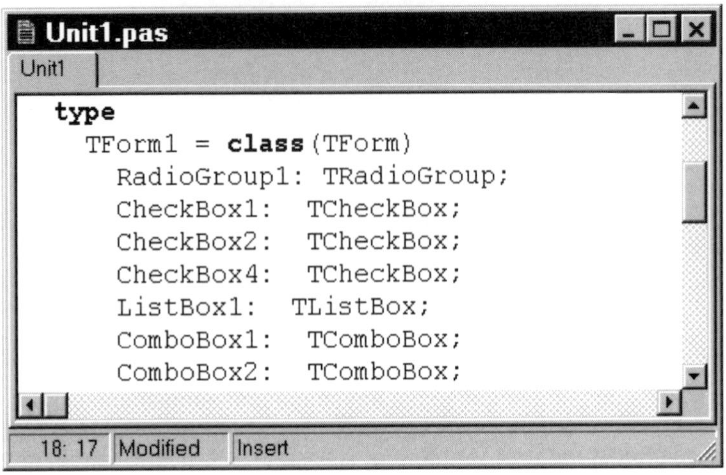

```
Unit1.pas                                    _ □ ×
Unit1
  type
    TForm1 = class(TForm)
      RadioGroup1: TRadioGroup;
      CheckBox1:  TCheckBox;
      CheckBox2:  TCheckBox;
      CheckBox4:  TCheckBox;
      ListBox1:   TListBox;
      ComboBox1:  TComboBox;
      ComboBox2:  TComboBox;

  18: 17  Modified   Insert
```

Fig. 6.9   *The unit module*

A professional looking user interface has been developed; if you are developing an application this is just the first stage – the data collected has to be stored and processed. You will see how this is done later.

7

Dialog Boxes

Introduction

Dialog boxes are used in Windows applications to display information and to accept limited input.

In this section you will learn about:

- Using standard dialog boxes.
- Creating customised dialog boxes.

The ShowMessage Procedure

The **ShowMessage** procedure is used to display a simple message to the user. A modal message box is displayed in response to the procedure call, for example as shown in fig. 7.1.

ShowMessage('This is displayed by the ShowMessage procedure');

Fig. 7.1
The *ShowMessage* procedure

The name of your applications executable file is used as the title.

If you want to display the dialog box in fig. 7.1, in response to a click on the left mouse button, you need to:

- Create a button by clicking on the **TButton** component in the Component Palette.
- Click on the form to place the button.
- Click on the Events page in the Object Inspector.
- Click on the **OnClick** event to go to the event handler for that event.

The template event handler is displayed:

```
procedure TForm1.Button1Click(Sender: TObject);
begin
   ...
end;
```

The **ShowMessage** procedure is called by inserting the following line between the *begin...end*:

```
ShowMessage('This is displayed by the ShowMessage procedure');
```

The dialog box appears in the centre of the screen. It automatically sizes itself so that it is big enough to display the message.

If you want to display the dialog box in a different position, you need to use the **ShowMessagePos** procedure. This is the same as the **ShowMessage** procedure except that the X and Y co-ordinates of the top left of the dialog box are specified, for example:

```
ShowMessagePos('This dialog box appears where you want it to', 200, 200);
```

If you want to display a message and also collect input, you need to use the **MessageDlg** function.

The MessageDlg Function

This function is more complicated than the **ShowMessage** procedure; however, it allows greater flexibility. The function call is:

```
Function MessageDlg(const Msg: string;
                    AType: TMsgDlgType;
                    AButtons: TMsgDlgButtons;
                    HelpCtx: LongInt) : Word;
```

Parameter	Meaning
Msg	The text in the message box.
AType	The type of dialog box.
AButtons	The types of buttons displayed in the dialog box.
HelpCtx	Link to a Help topic.

For example, to display the dialog box in fig. 7.2, the function call is:

MessageDlg('Unable to save file – disk full', mtError, [mbOk], 0);

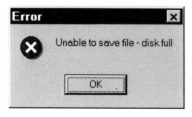

Fig. 7.2
The **MessageDlg** function

The *AButtons* parameter that determines the buttons displayed is a set, and therefore you have to specify the buttons to be displayed in [ ] brackets, for example [MbOk]. This allows you to list more than one button to be shown, for example [MbOk, MbCancel].

The constant **mtError** that displays the error graphic is defined as being of type **TMsgDlgType**. The other members are: **mtWarning, mtConfirmation, mtInformation** and **mtCustom,** and each displays a different caption and symbol. It is obvious from the names which caption is displayed.

The constant **mbOk** specifies the button to be displayed. The other members are **mbYes, mbNo, mbCancel, mbAbort, mbRetry, mbIgnore, mbAll** and **MbHelp.**

If you want to have more than one button (fig. 7.3), you can specify that in the function call; for example:

MessageDlg('Overwrite existing file?', mtWarning,[mbOk, mbCancel],0);

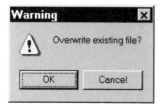

Fig. 7.3
Specifying more than one button
with the **MessageDlg** function

Since some common groupings of buttons occur, there is a short-hand way of specifying them:

MessageDlg('Delete all Files', mtConfirmation, mbYesNoCancel, 0);

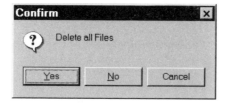

Fig. 7.4
Using pre-defined sets with
the **MessageDlg** function

In addition to **mbYesNoCancel** you can also use **mbOkCancel** and **mbAbortRetryIgnore**; note that you do not need to use the [ ] brackets here to define the set of buttons, since these constants are pre-defined sets (fig. 7.4).

The **MessageDlg** function positions the dialog box in the centre in the same way as the **ShowMessage** procedure. If you want to control its position you must use the **MessageDlgPos** function. This is the same as the **MessageDlg** function except that the X and Y co-ordinates of the top left of the dialog box are an additional two parameters.

Return Values from MessageDlg

The **MessageDlg** function returns a value that indicates which button has been clicked. The possible return values are: **mrNone**, **mrOk**, **mrCancel**, **mrAbort**, **mrRetry**, **mrIgnore**, **mrYes**, **mrNo** and **mrAll**.

Creating Input Forms

Dialog boxes can also be used to prompt for input, using two functions, **InputBox** and **InputQuery**.

The **InputBox** function is defined as:

*Function InputBox(const ACaption, APrompt, ADefault: **string**) : **string**;*

Parameter	Meaning
ACaption	The caption of the dialog box.
APrompt	The text adjacent to the edit box where the user types the input text.
ADefault	The text that is displayed in the edit box when the dialog box is first displayed.

If the user chooses OK, the value in the edit box is returned; however, if either the *Cancel* button is chosen or the **Escape** key is pressed, the string returned is equal to the *ADefault* parameter. The user cannot tell which button has been pressed.

If in addition to the string typed into the edit box the user needs to know which button was chosen, the **InputQuery** function must be used. The **InputQuery** function is:

*Function InputQuery(const ACaption, APrompt: **string**; var Value: **string**);*
   Boolean;

The **ACaption** and the **APrompt** parameters are the same as for the **InputBox** function; however, the *Value* variable is the default string parameter and a boolean value is returned to the user, which is true if the OK button is chosen and false if it is not. The text input is returned in the *Value* variable.

The dialog box shown in fig. 7.5 is a typical input box.

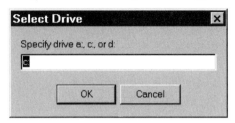

Fig. 7.5
The **InputQuery** function

It can be created by using this function call from the button click event handler, placed between the **begin...end** pair.

```
var
    drive : string;
begin
    drive := InputBox('Select Drive', 'Specify drive a:, c:, or d:', 'c:');
    ....
```

Custom Dialog Boxes

You can create a wide range of dialog boxes using **MessageDlg** and **InputBox**, but sometimes you want to prepare something which cannot be done with these functions. Delphi allows you to create custom dialog boxes. In fact, these are really just forms at design-time, but they have the same functionality and appear to the user as if they are dialog boxes. This is covered in the next chapter that looks at creating applications which have more than one form.

8

Using Forms

Introduction

Earlier chapters have looked at applications using only one form – which is created when you start a new project – but most applications have many forms.
  In this chapter you will learn about:

- Creating forms.
- Modal and modeless forms.
- Using form templates.

Modal and Modeless Forms

Forms can be either modal or modeless:

- A modal form must be closed before the focus can be switched to another window. You can do this either by clicking on the top left corner of the box or by clicking on one of the dialog box buttons and causing it to close itself. Most dialog boxes are modal.
- A modeless form allows the user to switch to another window.

At design-time, dialog boxes are neither modal or modeless; this property is controlled at run-time.

Form Templates

One important feature of Delphi is that it allows you to create libraries of reusable objects, such as forms. Delphi supplies a very useful library of form templates which can be used as the basis of your form. It is often easier to modify an existing form than to create a completely new form. To add a template form to your project:

- Select **New** from the **File** menu.
- The **New Items** dialog box is displayed.

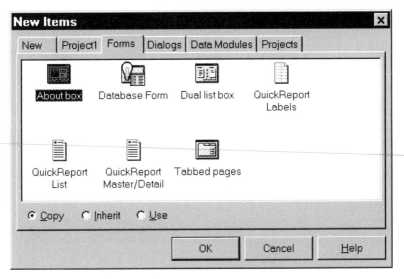

Fig. 8.1 *The New Items dialog box*

The **Forms** and **Dialogs** pages of the **New Items dialog** have a range of useful forms.

- Select either the **Forms** or **Dialogs** pages. Select the form you want and click on OK.

Delphi adds a copy of this form and all the associated files to your project. You can modify it without altering the template. Next we look at some of the most useful forms.

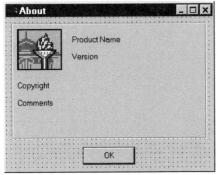
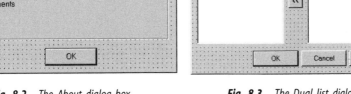

Fig. 8.2 *The About dialog box*   *Fig. 8.3* *The Dual list dialog box*

Initially these forms look complicated but, in fact, they are simply made up of the standard components that you have seen already. In the About dialog box (fig. 8.2) on the **Forms** page, the text *Product Name, Version, Copyright* and *Comments* are ordinary labels. The picture is an image box with a bit map providing the picture. These components are all on a **TPanel** component. The button is just an ordinary button.

The dual list dialog box on the **Forms** page allows you to select any of the items in the source list and transfers them to the destination list. The *Source* and *Destination* are list boxes (fig. 8.3). The buttons in between them are called speed buttons, which behave in exactly the same way as ordinary buttons except that a bit-map is used to provide an image on the button.

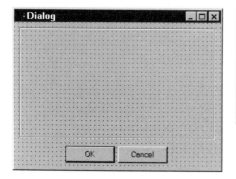

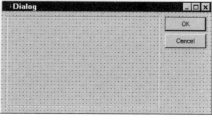

Fig. 8.4   *The Standard dialog box*   **Fig. 8.5**   *The alternative Standard dialog box*

The next two standard dialog boxes on the **Dialogs** page (fig. 8.4 and 8.5) are the same – the buttons are simply in a different place. The only other component apart from the buttons is a **TBevel** component which in this case appears as a bevelled box, although it can appear as a bevelled line.

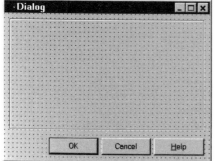

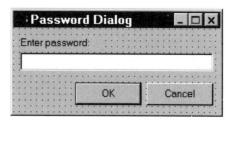

Fig. 8.6   *The Dialog with Help*   **Fig. 8.7**   *The Password dialog box*

There are two Dialog with Help boxes on the **Dialogs** page, one of which is shown in fig 8.6. They both consist of a **TBevel** component and three buttons. The

Password dialog (fig. 8.7) is a very useful dialog box used for reading passwords, and we shall look at it in more detail later in this chapter.

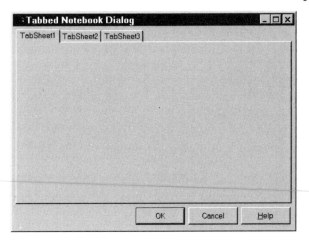

Fig. 8.8
The Tabbed Notebook dialog

The Tabbed Notebook dialog box (fig. 8.8), the Tabbed pages icon on the **Forms** page has three buttons and a **TPage Control** component. You can switch between each of the pages by clicking on the tags at the top of each page. Three pages are the default for this dialog box, but you can have as many pages as you want. The **TPage Control** component has become very popular in many recent applications and is a convenient way of making a large amount of data available. It is widely used in Delphi for example, in the Object Inspector.

After you have selected the style of new form that you want, there is a slight complication when you add a new form to a project; although the new form you have created is now available to the project, you need to specify which other forms are going to use this new form.

Allowing Forms to Use Each Other

When you add the form to your project, Delphi automatically makes an entry in the **uses** clause of the project file. You need to add the name of the new form to the **uses** section of the unit code of any form that wants to reference it.

The **uses** clause   ⟶

Fig. 8.9 *The **uses** clause*

The **uses** section (fig. 8.9) is at the top of the unit file, unit1.pas for the first form, unit2.pas for the second, and so on. If you fail to do this you get an error message displayed when you try to compile the program. In order to see the whole process of using an existing form from the Browse Gallery, the next example uses the Password dialog for specifying a password.

Password Input Dialog

The Password dialog box allows you to enter passwords without them being echoed on the screen as they are typed. To use this template:

- Select the **New Application** option from the **File** menu.
- Delphi creates a new project, including a single form. Add a button to this form.
- Select **New** on the **File** menu.
- When the **New Item** dialog is displayed, select the **Dialog** page, choose the **Password Dialog** option and click on **OK**.

The dialog box is displayed. The next stage is to write some Pascal that displays the dialog box when the button on the first form is clicked.

- Select the Events page from the Object Inspector.
- Double click on the **OnClick** event. This takes you to the event handler for the button click event.
- A line of Pascal is needed between the *begin...end*; pair to display the dialog box:

   PasswordDlg.ShowModal;

The **ShowModal** method is used to display a modal form.
   To show a modeless form use the **Show** method to display the form.
   If you try to compile and run the program at this stage, the identifier *PasswordDlg* is not recognised.

- Select the first form, called *Form1* by default and double click on it to go to the associated Pascal code.
- Add the name of the unit code associated with the Password dialog box, that is, the name of its unit identifier (unit2), to the **uses** clause of Form1.

The unit code associated with the first form is placed in a file called *unit1.pas*. The file name of the second unit code file is called *unit2.pas,* and so on. If you are unsure of the name of the file, double click on the form and the associated code is displayed with the name of the file in the window header (fig. 8.10).

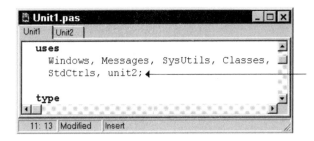

unit2 is the name
of the file
containing the
code associated
with the
Password dialog

Fig. 8.10 *Changing the **uses** clause*

- Select **Run** from the **Run** menu. This compiles and links the program before attempting to run it.

At run-time, when the button is clicked, the Password Dialog box (fig. 8.11) is displayed.

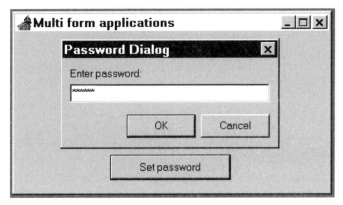

Fig. 8.11 *Multiple form applications*

When you type the password, only "*" is displayed.

This dialog box is in fact a group of components, one of them being an edit box where the password is entered. A property of edit boxes is **PasswordChar**, which in this case is set to "*". You can view this by displaying the Password dialog box and selecting the edit box on the dialog box. Make sure that the Properties page of the Object Inspector is displayed and find the **PasswordChar** property of the component.

Finding Forms and Units

If you are working with more than one form it can be confusing and difficult to find the form you want. You can display a list of forms in your project by choosing the **Forms** options from the **View** menu, as shown in fig. 8.12.

Fig. 8.12
Finding forms and units

You can view the form that you want by selecting it and then clicking on OK. To find and display any unit select the **Units** option from the **View** menu. If you wish to switch between the form and unit, you can select either the **Toggle Form/Unit** option from the **View** menu or press the short-cut key **F12**.

Saving Forms as Templates

If you create a form and think that you might to use it or something similar again, you can save it as a template.

- Click the right button on the mouse when it is over the form that you want to save as a template. This displays the SpeedMenu (fig. 8.13).

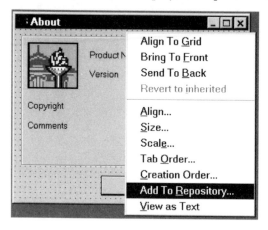

Fig. 8.13
The About box SpeedMenu

- Select the **Add to Repository** option. The Add to Repository dialog is displayed, as shown in fig. 8.14.
- The **Title** is a name for the template.
- The **Description** is a textual description of what the form does.
- The **Browse** button allows you to specify an icon that can be used to represent the form in the Repository.

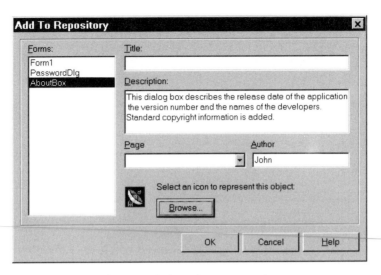

Fig. 8.14 *Saving a form as a template*

When you choose **OK**, the form is added to the Repository and appears as an option for this and subsequent projects.

Custom Dialog Boxes

Delphi offers a wide range of dialog boxes at run-time through the **ShowMessage**, **MessageDlg** and **InputBox** functions and at design-time through the New Items dialog; however, you may need to create your own dialog boxes which are just forms at design time. This application uses a custom dialog box to change the icon displayed in the picture box on the About Box.

- Select the **New Application** option from the **File** menu.
- Select **New** on the **File** menu.
- When the New Items dialog is displayed, select the **About Box** option from the **Forms** page and click on **OK**.
- Add an additional button to the dialog box and set its **Caption** property to *Change Icon*. The dialog box should look like that of fig. 8.15.
- This form should be the first one to appear when the program is run. To do this, select the **Options** option from the **Project** menu and set the main form to *AboutBox*.
- Next, create a second form by selecting the **New Form** option from the **File** menu.
- Add two buttons, an edit box, an image box and a **TOpenDialog** component. The form should look something like the one shown in fig. 8.16.

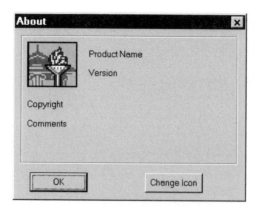

Fig. 8.15
The About box

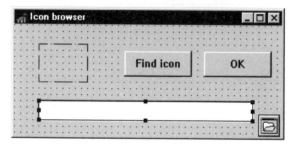

Fig. 8.16
The Icon browser

The **TOpenDialog** component is on the **Dialogs** page of the Component Palette, and is a standard way of browsing through your directories to find a file. It does not matter where you put it on the form, since it is invisible at run-time.

To display the *Icon Browser* dialog box when the *Change Icon* button is pressed, two changes need to be made to the code:

- In the click event for the *Change Icon* button add the line:

  form2.ShowModal.

- In the **uses** clause add the name *form2.*
- Add the name *AboutBox* to the **uses** clause of *form2.*

If you run the program now, the *About* dialog is displayed first. When you click on the *Change Icon* button the *Icon Browser* dialog box is displayed, but more code is needed in order to find and select the required icon.

The OpenFile Dialog Box

The **TOpenDialog** component is used to select the file. The **Execute** method has to be used to display this dialog box.

You need to add the line:

Opendialog1.Execute;

to the click event for the *Find Icon* button on the *Icon Browser* dialog box.

The **Open File** common dialog box has a **Filter** property which specifies the types of files to be displayed. In this case you only want to display files with an extension of ICO.

Click on the **Filter** property and the **Filters Editor** (fig. 8.17) is displayed.

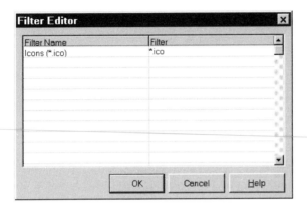

Fig. 8.17
The Filters editor

Enter a **Filter Name** of *Icons (*.ico)* and a **Filter** of *.ico.

When you run the program now and click on the *Find Icon* button, the **TOpenDialog** component displays the Open dialog box which allows you to browse through your disks and directories. The dialog box is shown in fig. 8.18.

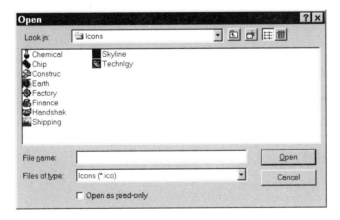

Fig. 8.18   *The Open dialog box.*

The **FileName** property of the **TOpenDialog** component is the name of the currently selected file.

To display the name of this file in the edit box, you need to add one line to the event handler for the *Find Icon* button after executing the Open dialog box:

*Edit1.**Text** := Opendialog1.**FileName**;*

To display the icon in the picture box, the **LoadFromFile** method is used after the name of the picture has been put into the edit box:

*image1.**Picture.LoadFromFile**(Opendialog1.**FileName**);*

The completed *Icon Browser* form should look like the one shown in fig. 8.19.

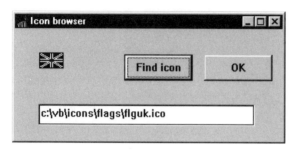

Fig. 8.19
The completed icon browser

When you are satisfied with the image, click on the *OK* button to return to the *About* box (fig. 8.20). You need to add the following two lines of code to the event handler for the *OK* button:

*aboutbox.image1.**Picture** := form2.image1.**Picture**;*
*aboutbox.**ShowModal**;*

This code assigns the **Picture** property of the **TImage** component called *image1* on *form2* to the **Picture** property of the **TImage** component, also called *image1* on the About box dialog. It is acceptable for the two image boxes to have the same name since they are on different forms, but in order to refer to a component on a different form, you need to specify the name of that form first.

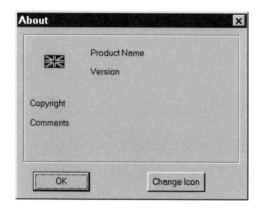

Fig. 8.20
The updated About box

This completes the application which has looked at using and modifying a standard common dialog box and at creating a new custom dialog box. The interaction between forms or dialog boxes is fairly straightforward, but it is unlike most other aspects of Delphi in that you have explicitly to declare in the **uses** section of the unit code of a form which other forms are referred to.

9

MDI Forms

Introduction

Multiple Documents Interface (MDI) forms allow a parent form to open child windows within the parent window. Single Document Interface (SDI) forms only have a parent window. Delphi only allows you to have one MDI parent form, but you can have as many child forms as you wish.

In this chapter you will learn about:

- Creating and Using MDI forms
- Tiling and cascading MDI forms.

The FormStyle Property

Forms have a property called **FormStyle** (fig. 9.1), which is used to determine if a form is SDI or MDI. The **FormStyle** property has four possible values:

Value	Meaning
fsNormal	The form an SDI form.
fsMDIForm	The form is an MDI parent form.
fsMDIChild	The form is an MDI child form.
fsStayOnTop	The form is SDI and stays on top of all other open forms.

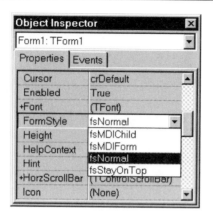

Fig. 9.1
The **FormStyle** property

Creating Parent and Child Forms

In order to create a parent form and three child forms:

- Start a new project.
- Use the **New Form** option from the **File** menu to create three new blank forms, in addition to the first automatically created form.
- Select the **Forms** option from the **View** menu and select *form1*. This displays the form first created. This is going to be the MDI parent form.
- Click on the Properties page of the Object Inspector and set the **FormStyle** property to **fsMDIForm**.
- Select the other three forms in turn and set their **FormStyle** properties to **fsMDIChild**.

Unit1.pas is the supporting code module for *Form1*, unit2.pas for *Form2*, and so on.

- Add unit2, unit3 and unit4 to the **uses** clause of unit1.pas (fig. 9.2), otherwise any references to say *Form1* from unit2, unit3, or unit4 will not be recognised.

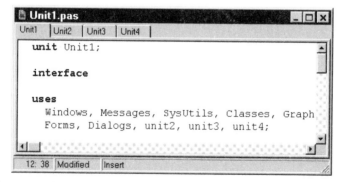

Fig. 9.2

If no Pascal code is written and the application is run, all three of the child forms are shown cascaded on the parent form (fig 9.3).

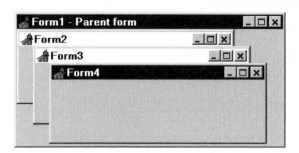

Fig. 9.3
Cascading the child forms

Auto-Creation of Forms

The main project form is always created, that is, it is loaded into the computer's memory when the application is run. Any other forms that are used in the project are also automatically created at run-time. In addition, if the main form is an MDI form, the child forms are also displayed within the parent. The advantages of doing this is that if a form is already in memory, it can be displayed far more quickly than if it has to be loaded into memory from disk when it has to be displayed. The application initially takes longer to get started, but should then run faster – provided that you have enough memory.

If you want to stop forms from being loaded in memory, you have explicitly to tell Delphi.

- Chose **Options** from the **Project** menu and select the **Forms** page.

Fig. 9.4
Auto-creation of forms

- To move *Form2*, *Form3* and *Form4* from the *Auto-create forms* list, select each in turn and press the button with the single right-pointing arrow on it.

The selected form is moved to the right-hand list (fig. 9.4) and is automatically created at run-time. If you want to move all entries from the *Auto-create forms* list, click on the button with the double right-pointing arrow. Similarly use the single and double-left pointing arrows to move forms back to the *Auto-create forms* list.

The main form can also be changed in this menu by using the list at the top of this dialog box.

When this change is made and the application is run, just *Form1* is displayed.

Displaying Child Forms

To display child forms, the forms must be loaded into memory at run-time or using Delphi jargon "instantiated". This is a fairly straightforward procedure, but every stage must be followed, otherwise the program will fail to compile.

The unit file of the main form, *Form1*, must be edited, and the **uses** clause must have the name of the unit files for forms, *Form2*, *Form3* and *Form4*, added; that is *unit2*, *unit3* and *unit4*.

> *uses*
> *SysUtils, WinTypes, WinProcs, Messages, Classes, Graphics, Controls, Forms, Dialogs, unit2, unit3, unit4;*

The **var** clause must have the name of the form followed by the type of the form. This creates an identifier of a specified type. Multiple instances of the same type can be created.

> *var*
>   *Form1: TForm1;*
>   *Form2: TForm2;*
>   *Form3: TForm3;*
>   *Form4: TForm4;*

To load the form into memory, the **Create** method is used for each form between the *begin.. end* of the event handler for the **OnClick** event for the form.

> *procedure TForm1.FormClick(Sender: TObject);*
> *begin*
>   *Form2 := Tform2.**Create**(Self);*
>   *Form3 := Tform3.**Create**(Self);*
>   *Form4 := Tform4.**Create**(Self);*
>   *Form2.**Show**;*
>   *Form3.**Show**;*
>   *Form4.**Show**;*
> *end;*

When this application is run, *Form1* is displayed. When the mouse is clicked over this form, the other three forms are also displayed. The use of the reserved word **Self** is optional and can be omitted, leaving just ( ).

Tiling Child Forms

By default the child forms are cascaded. If you want to tile them vertically or horizontally, use the **Tile** method after first setting the **TileMode** to either **tbVertical** (fig. 9.5) or **tbHorizontal** (fig. 9.6). For example:

TileMode := tbVertical;
Tile;

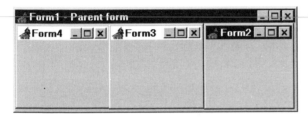

Fig. 9.5
TileMode is tbVertical

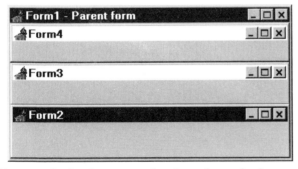

Fig. 9.6
TileMode is tbHorizontal

To cascade the forms use the **Cascade** method.

Note: you can only use the **Tile** and **Cascade** methods for MDI forms that have child forms.

10

Menus

Introduction

Menus are an important way of grouping commands together. Menus are often used to display a range of common dialog boxes for frequently used operations such as changing colour, opening files and changing fonts. In this chapter you will learn about:

- Using the Menu Designer.
- Using the Menu Designer SpeedMenu.
- Creating menus.
- Using the Color and Fonts dialog boxes.

The Menu Designer

The Menu Designer allows you to design both main menus and pop-up menus. Main menus are attached to a forms title bar, while a pop-up menu appears in response to pressing the right button of the mouse.

To start the Menu Designer, click on either the **TMainMenu** or the **TPopUp-Menu** components on the Standard page of the Component Palette.

Designing Main Menus

To start designing a main menu, click on the **TMainMenu** component and then click on the form. The **TMainMenu** component is displayed (fig. 10.1). It does not matter where it is placed, since it is not be visible at run-time.

Fig. 10.1 *The **TMainMenu** component*

In order to design the menu you can either:

- Double click on the **TMainMenu** icon

or

- Select the **TMainMenu** icon and then click on the three dots on the right of the **Items** property in the Object Inspector.

The design window (fig. 10.2) is displayed.

The menu bar ⟶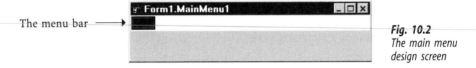

Fig. 10.2
*The main menu
design screen*

The Caption and Name Properties

Every item in a menu, both those displayed in the menu bar and those that appear when the user clicks on the menu bar have **Caption** and **Name** properties. The **Caption** property is the text that is displayed in the menu, while the **Name** property is how the programmer refers to that menu item in Pascal code. When the design window appears, the user is automatically prompted for the first item in the menu bar. As this is typed, it appears in the **Caption** property shown in the Object Inspector. For example, when the menu designer appears, type *File*. This is shown in the **Caption** property. If you press the **Enter** key, the word *File* appears as the first item on the menu bar on the form being designed, as shown in fig. 10.3. Every item in the menu must have a **Name**; however, you do not have to set it explicitly. If you click on the *File* entry in the menu designer, the properties associated with it are displayed in the Object Inspector. In this case, Delphi has created the name *File1*. You can change either the **Name** or **Caption** properties at any time if you wish.

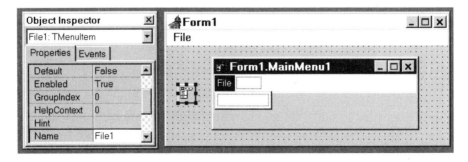

Fig. 10.3 *Creating a main menu*

Adding, Inserting and Deleting Menu Items

- To add a new menu item, run the menu designer, click on the position that you want the item to go to and type the text that you want displayed on the menu. This appears in the **Caption** property displayed in the Object Inspector. Next press **Enter**. When you have added an item to a menu, it is available in the form that you are designing.
- To insert a new item in the middle of a list, position the cursor on the menu item after the point where you want to place the new item, then press the right mouse button. Choose the **Insert** option from the SpeedMenu, then continue as before.
- To delete a menu item, position the cursor on the item in the menu designer and press the **Delete** key.

Menu items can also dragged by the mouse to change their position in the menu system.

Separator Bars, Accelerator and Short-cut Keys

Separator bars are useful for putting a line between items. They are menu items that have a hyphen as their **Caption**.

When you become proficient in using an application, you often want to use accelerator keys rather than the menu; for example, to invoke the **File** menu, on most applications you can type **Alt+F**. You can see in fig. 10.4 that the **F** of the word **File** is underlined. In order for your application to do this, insert an ampersand (&) character before the letter that you have chosen to be the accelerator key. It need not be the first letter.

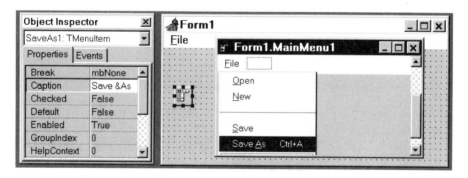

Fig. 10.4   *Short-cut and accelerator keys*

Short-cut keys are similar to accelerator keys in that they allow you to choose a menu item from the keyboard. You can specify a short-cut key by setting the **Shortcut** property of the menu item to the key you have chosen in the Object

Inspector. When you have chosen a short-cut key, this appears adjacent to the caption of this menu item when it is displayed.

Note: Delphi does not check for duplicates in either accelerator or short-cut keys – you need to do this yourself.

Creating Sub Menus

Sub menus or nested menus allow the application to provide a list of options from a single menu item. For example, if there are a list of menu items relating to formatting text, next to an entry specifying **Size**, it is useful to have a further menu that provides a list of these sizes (fig. 10.5).

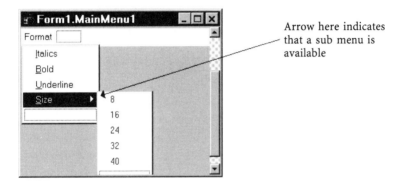

Arrow here indicates that a sub menu is available

Fig. 10.5   *Creating sub menus*

The finished menu item is shown in fig. 10.6; the blank entries at the bottom of the menus are not shown in the menu when the application is run.

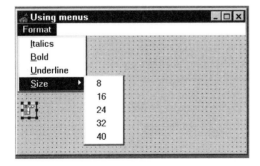

Fig. 10.6
The menu on the design screen

The menu usually appears at run-time as it appears on the design screen that is, below the menu bar; however, if there is not enough room on the screen to display it below, it is displayed above the menu bar. This level of functionality is typical of the thoroughness with which Delphi has been designed. It really does simplify the problems of developing software in a Windows environment.

To create a nested menu, position the cursor on the item that is to have the sub menu and press **Ctrl→**. A small arrow head appears against this item. The items in the sub menu are entered, amended and deleted in the same way as other menu items.

Designing Pop-up Menus

To start designing a pop-up menu, click on the **TPopUpMenu** component (fig. 10.7).

Fig. 10.7   *The **TPopUpMenu** component*

Click on the form to insert the menu and then double click on the **TPopUp-Menu** component. The design window is displayed (fig. 10.8).

Fig. 10.8
The pop-up menu design screen

Pop-up menus are very similar to main menus except that they do not have a menu bar. The way in which items are inserted, amended and deleted is the same. Pop-up menus appear when the right button of the mouse is clicked. In order for this to work, the **AutoPop** property needs to be set to true, this is the default. In addition you need to assign the **PopUpMenu** property of the form that you want to display the menu to the name of the pop-up menu.

The **Alignment** property of the pop-up menu is useful in controlling where the menu appears in relation to the position of the mouse when it is clicked.

Property value	Meaning
paLeft	Top left corner of the menu is placed at the mouse location.
paRight	Top right corner of the menu is placed at the mouse location.
paCenter	Top centre of the menu is placed at the mouse location.

If there is not enough room on your screen to display your menu fully, Delphi does the best it can.

The Menu Designer Speed Menu

The SpeedBar displays the most common features of the Menu Designer. To display the SpeedBar (fig. 10.9), right click when the cursor is on the Menu Designer window.

Fig. 10.9
The menu designer SpeedMenu

Using Menu Templates

Most applications have standard menus for dealing with files, changing the window being displayed and for getting help. To save creating these every time you begin an application, you can use menu templates. Some are provided by Delphi and are in the /DELPHI/BIN directory with an extension of DMT (Delphi Menu Template), but you can also create your own.

If you want to use an existing menu template:

- Run the menu designer.
- Run the SpeedMenu for the designer by right clicking on the right mouse while it is over the designer.
- Choose the **Insert From Template** option. The Insert template window is shown in fig. 10.10.

Fig. 10.10
Using an existing menu

- Select the template that you want by either double clicking on it or by selecting it and pressing **Enter**.

If you want to delete a template, choose the **Delete Templates** option from the SpeedBar as shown in fig. 10.11.

Fig. 10.11
Deleting menu templates

One of the most common templates is the File Menu template, which offers all the standard Windows options.

Creating Menu Templates

Any menu you create can be saved as a template. In order to save the menu:

- Click on the right mouse button over the Menu Designer to run the SpeedMenu.
- Choose the **Save As Template** option.
- The Save Template dialog box is displayed as shown in fig. 10.12.

Fig. 10.12
Saving menu templates

- If you wish, you can enter a brief description of the template in the *Template Description* section; this is just to help you remember what the template does.

- Click on **OK** to save the template.

Connecting Menu Events and Code

The best way of learning about a feature of Delphi is to try and develop a program using that feature. This section looks at developing an application for changing the style of text in a memo box using a menu and sub menus. You also look at using two common dialog boxes for choosing the font of the text and the background colour of the text box.

- First create a new project and give the form a suitable caption – I have chosen *Chameleon.*
- Create a memo box and double click on the **Lines** property of this component. The text displayed in the memo box is contained in this property. Set this to *Chameleon,* or to any other text that you want.
- The next stage is to create the menu. Click on the **TMainMenu** component which is on the Standard page of the Component Palette. It does not matter where on the form that you position this component, since it is not visible at run-time.
- Double click on the component and you go to the menu design screen.
- The first menu header is *Format.* The menu items under *Format* are *Italics, Bold, Underline* and *Size.*
- The second menu header is *Colour* and has two items, *Memo colour* and *Font colour.* The *Memo colour* is the background colour of the memo box, while the *Font colour* is the colour of the letters in the box.

At this stage your menu design screen should look like that of fig. 10.13.

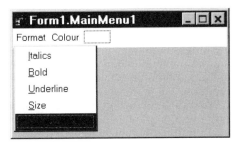

Fig. 10.13
The menu design screen

There needs to be a sub menu under the *Size* option – to allow you to select the size of text that you want in the memo box. To create this sub menu, click the right mouse button over the *Size* option and the menu shown in fig. 10.14 is displayed.

Click on the **Create Submenu** option and type in the possible font sizes as 8, 12, 16, 24, 32 and 40.

If you return to your main form, the menu is now in place – and you can run the program which has a complete menu system – the only drawback is that nothing yet happens to the text in the memo box. Some code needs to be written for this.

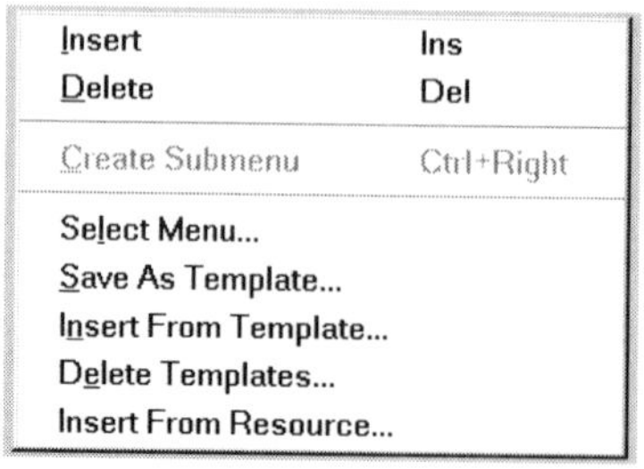

Insert	Ins
Delete	Del
Create Submenu	Ctrl+Right
Select Menu...	
Save As Template...	
Insert From Template...	
Delete Templates...	
Insert From Resource...	

Fig. 10.14
The menu designer SpeedMenu

If you click on the *Italic* entry in the table in the design form, you go to the template code for dealing with this event. To make the text italic you need to add one line of code to the event handler:

memo1.Font.Style := [fsItalic];

However, you need to add more code if you want this menu item to toggle between italic and non-italic. In addition you need to check to see if the text is bold. There are four possibilities to consider:

- If the text is italic, make it non-italic.
- If the text is non-italic, make it italic.
- If the text is italic and bold, make it bold only.
- If the text is non-italic and bold, make it bold and italic.

The code for doing this looks like the code shown.

```
procedure TForm1.Italics1Click(Sender: TObject);
begin
    if (memo1.Font.Style = [fsItalic]) then
        memo1.Font.Style := []            {if text is italic make it non-italic}
    else
    if (memo1.Font.Style = []) then
        memo1.Font.Style := [fsItalic];   {if not italic make italic}

    if (memo1.Font.Style = [fsbold, fsitalic]) then
        memo1.Font.Style := [fsbold]      {if bold + italic make bold only}
    else
    if (memo1.Font.Style = [fsbold]) then
        memo1.Font.Style := [fsbold, fsitalic];   {if bold make bold + italic}
end;
```

You need similar code in the event handler that deals with the *Bold* menu option.

All the code for dealing with the selection of a menu item is dealt with in the click event for that item, similarly there are click events for making the code bold or for underlining it.

You create the code for changing the size in the same way. Click on the menu item that you want to write the code for, and you will go to the outline code that Delphi creates for you. The code that you need for changing the size of the text to 8 point is:

```
procedure TForm1.N81Click(Sender: TObject);
begin
    memo1.Font.Size := 8;
end;
```

You need similar code for changing the size to the other values. The running program should look like that of fig. 10.15.

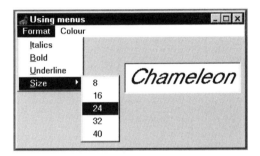

Fig. 10.15
The running program

The Font Dialog Box

If you want to change one aspect of the text at a time, this is permissible; but often you want to change several aspects, including the font, size and characteristics such as underlining and embolding. Delphi provides an easy way of doing this using a common dialog box.

The **TFontDialog** component is not only easy to use, but gives your applications a professional look. You need to include the **TFontDialog** component in your design form. It is on the Dialogs page of the Component Palette. To display this dialog box, you need to use the **Execute** method by putting a line of code in the event handler for the *Font* menu header:

```
procedure TForm1.Font1Click(Sender: TObject);
begin
    fontdialog1.Execute;
end;
```

When you run the program and click on **Font** the font dialog box (fig. 10.16) is displayed.

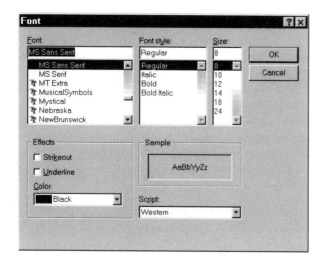

Fig. 10.16
The **TFontDialog** component

You can change all the features of the text using this dialog box. To commit those changes to the memo box, a single statement is needed after the **Execute** statement:

   *memo1.****Font*** := *fontdialog1.****Font****;*

The **Font** property contains all the sub properties such as underlining, embolding and size.

One minor problem with this dialog box is that a set of default characteristics is displayed, the font is **System**, the size is 10, and so on. If you want the dialog box to display the characteristics of the memo box font, a bit more code is needed.

The whole event handler looks like this:

   procedure *TForm1.Font1Click(Sender: TObject);*
   begin
       *fontdialog1.****Font*** := *memo1.****Font****;*
       *fontdialog1.****Execute****;*
       *memo1.****Font*** := *fontdialog1.****Font****;*
   end;

The TColorDialog Component

To change the colour of the memo box and the text, another dialog box can be used: the **TColorDialog** component (the spelling of this component is always difficult for British Delphi programmers) This is also on the Dialogs page of the Component Palette.

The event handler for the *Memo Colour* option and the *Font colour* option is:

```
procedure TForm1.Memocolor1Click(Sender: TObject);
begin
     colordialog1.Execute;
     memo1.Color := colordialog1.Color;
end;

procedure TForm1.Fontcolor1Click(Sender: TObject);
begin
     colordialog1.Execute;
     memo1.Font.Color := colordialog1.Color;
end;
```

When you run the program and click on either option, the dialog box is displayed (fig. 10.17). Click on the colour that you want and then on the **OK** button.

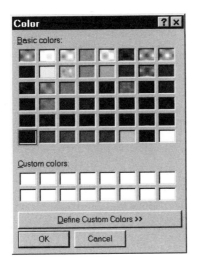

Fig. 10.17
The **TColorDialog** component

It is straightforward in Delphi to create menus, and for frequently used operations there is a good selection of common dialog boxes that give your application a professional feel. Some third parties are developing additional dialog boxes and components for Delphi (there has been a thriving market in this area for Visual Basic controls for several years). As well as looking good and being reliable, they are also easy to use – if possible you should always use them in preference to your own custom-made dialogs.

11
Debugging

Introduction

Everyone writes programs with bugs, which either cause the program to crash or to behave in an unexpected way. Delphi has an excellent debugger as a part of the development environment. If you are not used to using this sort of debugger it is tempting to continue with other (less efficient!) methods, but it is very worthwhile spending the time to become proficient in using the Delphi debugger. In this chapter you will learn how to:

- Include debugging information in your application.
- Halt program execution using breakpoints.
- View and modify data values at breakpoints.
- Step through programs.
- Trace programs.

Run-time and Logic Errors

If your program cannot be understood by the Delhi compiler, Delphi will tell you where the error has occurred and give you a chance to correct it. There are 198 possible compiler errors, such as missing brackets and identifiers not being recognised. If you want to see the definitive list, use the **Index** option of the Delphi **Help** to find *error messages*. The most common errors at this stage are *unknown identifier*, that is, you have used an identifier and not declared it, and syntax errors. The most common syntax error, particularly for inexperienced Pascal programmers, is forgetting to put a semicolon at the end of the line. Errors that occur at compile time are usually straightforward to fix.

There are two main types of errors apart from compiler errors:

- Run-time errors
- Logic errors.

Run-time errors occur when the syntax of your program is correct and it can be successfully built, but for some reason does not execute properly; for example, if you try and divide by zero, or try to open a file that does not exist. When an error is detected at run-time, program execution is halted. The debugger will tell you where the error has occurred.

A dialog box is displayed when a run-time error occurs, giving you information about the error, as shown in fig. 11.1.

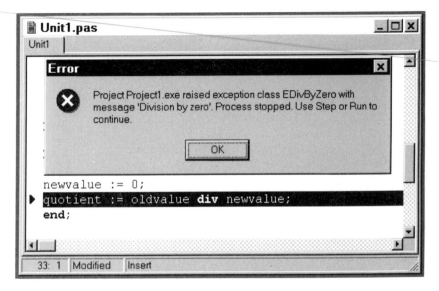

Fig. 11.1   *Delphi error messages*

The unit file where the error has occurred is also displayed with the error line highlighted. You have the option to examine the program more closely using the debugger.

Logic errors are errors that cause the program to behave in unexpected ways without actually crashing. These are often very difficult to detect; however, the debugger can be of help here as well, by allowing you to step slowly through the program and find the point at which the program starts to behave differently from the way in which you expect.

Using the Debugger

When you compile and link your application, Delphi needs to produce a great deal of information that allows it to relate the executable form of the program (the EXE file) with the source files. If there is a run-time error and this debug information is not available, you will not be able to find the line of your source code where the error has occurred. The debugger also relates the data in the EXE file, which is stored as a series of bytes, to the high-level data structures, such as integers and floating point numbers, which are used in the source files. Without this information it is impossible to establish a link between the Pascal code, its data and the machine code of the EXE file.

To use the debugger you need to instruct the compiler to include this information in the EXE file:

- Choose the **Options** option from the **Projects** menu.
- Click on the **Compiler** page.

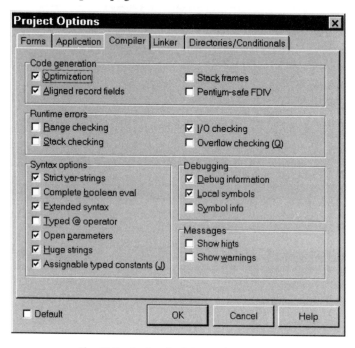

Fig. 11.2   *Setting the Debug options to "on"*

- Turn on all three of the debugging check boxes (fig. 11.2).

The debug information can be stored either in a separate file with a DCU extension if you want to use the internal debugger, or alternatively, if you wish to use the standalone Turbo debugger, the debug information must be included in the EXE file. Select the **Linker** page of the **Projects Options** menu and click on the *"Include TDW dialog info"* check box. This chapter concentrates on the use of the internal debugger.

Generating debug information significantly reduces the speed and increases the size of the EXE file, especially if all the debug information is included in the EXE file. It is usual to use the debugger when developing, but remove all debug information when the application is working satisfactorily, particularly if it is to be distributed to a customer.

Stopping Program Execution

The debugger allows you to run the program in the normal way until it reaches a point that you specify in the program. When the program halts at this point, you can examine the value of identifiers and see if they are what you expect. You can specify the point at which your program stops in two ways:

- Select a line of code that the program will run to.
- Use breakpoints.

There are three ways of specifying the line of code, either

- Click on the right mouse button, while the mouse is over the code editor window, to display the speed menu and select the **Run to Cursor** option

or

- Choose the **Run to Cursor** option from the **Run** menu (fig. 11.3)

or

- Press **F4**.

Close Page	Ctrl+F4
Open File at Cursor	Ctrl+Enter
New Edit Window	
Browse Symbol at Cursor	
Topic Search	F1
Toggle Breakpoint	F5
Run to Cursor	
Evaluate/Modify...	
Add Watch at Cursor...	Ctrl+F5
View As Form	Alt+F12
Read Only	
Message View	
Properties	

Fig. 11.3
*Choose the **Run to Cursor** option from the SpeedMenu*

When the program is run, it goes at full speed until it hits the stop point. The one disadvantage with using this method is that you can only specify one stop point in the program. If you want to have more than one stop point, you need to use breakpoints.

Setting Breakpoints

Breakpoints must be set on executable lines of code; if they are set on comments or other non-executable lines, they are never reached. Breakpoints can be set either before or at run-time.

To set a breakpoint, find the point in the code where you want the program to break and then you can do either of the following:

- Click on the left of a line in the code editor – the line will be highlighted

or

- Bring up the SpeedMenu for the code editor and select **Toggle Breakpoint**

or

- Press **F5**.

There are other ways of setting breakpoints, but these three are the easiest.

Restarting After Breakpoints

When the program execution has been suspended, and you want to restart it, select **Run** from the **Run** menu or use the SpeedMenu. If you want to continue execution a line at a time, use the **Trace Into** or **Step Over** options from the **Run** menu as described later in this chapter.

If you want to run the program again from the beginning, choose the **Program Reset** option from the **Run** option.

Viewing Breakpoints

It can be difficult to keep track of your breakpoints in a complicated debugging session, but Delphi does help in this. When a breakpoint is chosen, the lines of code in the code editor are highlighted.

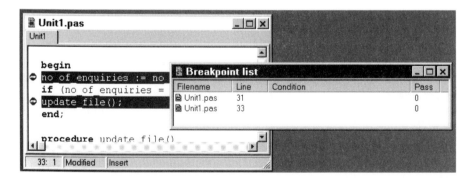

Fig. 11.4   *The Breakpoint list*

In addition if you choose the **Breakpoints** option from the **View** menu, a list of breakpoints is displayed (fig. 11.4).

Using Breakpoints

If you want to move quickly between breakpoints, you can select the breakpoint that you want to go to in the Breakpoint list and then bring up the SpeedMenu by clicking the right mouse button.

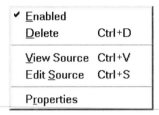

Fig. 11.5
Moving between breakpoints

Select the **View Source** option to move to that breakpoint in the code editor. If you choose this option, the Breakpoint list window retains the focus; if you choose the **Edit Source** option, the code editor window is given the focus.

Disabling, Enabling and Deleting Breakpoints

Sometimes you may want the program to ignore a particular breakpoint. You can disable breakpoints by:

- Opening the Breakpoint list dialog
- Highlighting the breakpoint that you want to disable
- Clicking on the **Enabled** option from the SpeedMenu.

If you want to enable a disabled breakpoint, choose the **Enabled** option again from the SpeedMenu when the breakpoint is highlighted.

If you want to disable or enable all breakpoints, choose the appropriate option from the SpeedMenu.

If you decide that a breakpoint is no longer needed, you can delete it. This is done as follows.

- Find the breakpoint that you want to delete in the code editor.
- Display the SpeedMenu.
- Choose the **Toggle Breakpoint** option or press the short-cut key **F5**.

Alternatively:

- Click on the stop sign in the code editor window, or
- Delete all breakpoints using Breakpoint list dialog's SpeedMenu.

There are other ways of deleting breakpoints, but the ones described here are the easiest to use.

Conditional Breakpoints

Normally when you are using a breakpoint, you want the program to stop every time that it reaches it but, in some circumstances, you may want the breakpoint to be ignored. If, for example, you have a loop where the loop counter goes from 1 to 500, and you only want the program to stop when the loop counter reaches 500, you need to associate a condition with the breakpoint. When the condition is met, the program will stop running at the breakpoint.

You set a conditional breakpoint by:

- Creating a breakpoint in the usual way
- Displaying the Breakpoint list window, by choosing the **Breakpoints** option from the **View** menu
- Select the breakpoint whose properties you want to change and choose the **Properties** option from the SpeedMenu
- The Edit breakpoint dialog box is then displayed (fig. 11.6).

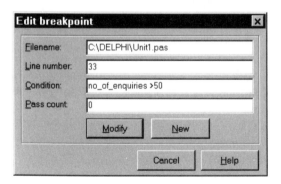

Fig. 11.6
The Edit breakpoint dialog box

The condition box can have an expression that is calculated every time the breakpoint is reached. When the condition is met, the program stops at the breakpoint. In the example shown, the program stops when the integer variable *no_of_enquiries* is greater than 50. If you want to put a condition into this box, just select it and then type it in the usual way.

The *Pass Count* gives the number of times that the line of code the breakpoint is on must be executed before the program stops; for example, if it is set to 10, it is decremented each time this line is reached until it gets to 1. The program will then stop.

You can use either the *Conditions* option or the *Pass count* option, or both for setting a conditional breakpoint.

Stepping

If you want to examine how the program behaves line after line, you can put a breakpoint on every line, but a better way is to use the **Trace Into** and **Step Over** commands. These commands execute one line of code at a time, pausing after each one.

The **Trace Into** command executes a line at a time. When it encounters a procedure or function call, if there is debug information available for that module it steps into it and executes it one line at a time. When the end of the module is reached, the debugger steps back to the calling module.

To carry out a trace either:

• Select the **Trace Into** option from then **Run** menu

or

• Press **F7**

or

• Click on the **Trace** button on the SpeedBar.

The **Step Over** command is very similar to the **Trace Into** command except that when a procedure or function call is reached, that module is executed without any pauses (unless you have placed a breakpoint in it). The program pauses at the line after the module call. Sometimes when you are sure that the called module will not produce any errors, it is best to step over rather than laboriously stepping through it.

To carry out the **Step Over** command:

• Select the **Step Over** option from then **Run** menu

or

• Press **F8**

or

• Click on the **Step Over** button on the SpeedBar.
It is easiest to use the buttons on the SpeedBar.

Pausing Programs

If there is a logic error in your program, you may want to pause its execution. The **Program Pause** option on the **Run** menu does this. You can later continue program execution in the same way as if a breakpoint had been reached.

If you find that you cannot interrupt your program, press **Ctrl+Alt+Del** to stop the program. You may need to do this more than once, since this command is not acknowledged if the Windows kernel is executing.

If you decide that you want to stop running the program, choose the **Program Reset** option from the **Run** menu.

Using the SpeedBar

Delphi has four SpeedBar buttons, shown in fig. 11.7, which provide a quick way of using some of the most common functions found in the **Run** menu.

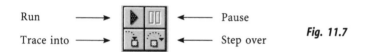

Run   ⟶   ⟵   Pause

Trace into   ⟶   ⟵   Step over   *Fig. 11.7*

- The **Run** button is equivalent to the **Run** option.
- The **Pause** button is equivalent to the **Program Pause** option.
- The **Trace Into** button is equivalent to the **Trace Into** option.
- The **Step Over** button is equivalent to the **Step Over** option.

Viewing Data

When the program has stopped execution, either as a result of a breakpoint or because you are stepping through it, you can examine data values in the program.

Watches can be used to monitor the value of a variable constantly while the program is executing. Every time the value being watched changes, it is updated in a Watch window.

There are several ways to set a watch, but the simplest is to:

- Click on right button to view the code editor's SpeedMenu.
- Select the **Add Watch at Cursor** option.

The **Watch Properties** window is then displayed (fig. 11.8).

The expression is evaluated and displayed as the program executes. In this case the value of the integer variable *no_of_enquiries* is displayed. When the program is executed, the Watch List window is displayed with the current values of the expression at that time.

In fig. 11.9 there are two variables being evaluated.

The expression is not limited to a single identifier name. It can be anything that can form the right-hand side of an assignment statement.

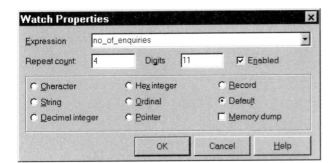

Fig. 11.8
The Watch Properties window

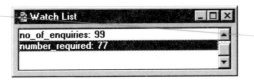

Fig. 11.9
The Watch List window

If you want to delete or disable a watch, select that option from the **Watch List** SpeedMenu. This SpeedMenu also allows you to delete or disable all watches.

Modifying Variables

In addition to viewing variables, it is also straightforward to change their values. When the program has paused, display the SpeedMenu for the code editor and select the **Evaluate/Modify** option. This displays the dialog box shown in fig. 11.10.

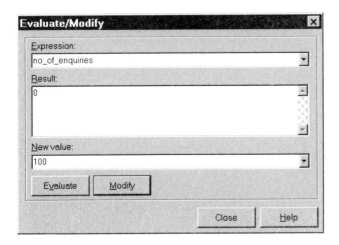

Fig. 11.10
Modifying and evaluating expressions

- Enter the name of the identifier or expression that you want to evaluate in the **Expression** edit box.

- Click **Evaluate** to calculate the present value.
- Enter the new value into edit box.
- Click on **Modify** to update the expression.

When the program continues executing, it uses the new value specified.

Using the Debugger

The debugging facilities available in Delphi offer all the features that you could possibly want; this is both an advantage and a disdvantage. When learning a powerful new development environment such as Delphi, there seems to be so much to learn that the debugger may seem to be one thing that you can leave until later. This is fine in the short term, but it is better to learn about these facilities as soon as you have time. If you wait until there is a bug that you cannot find any other way and the debugging tools are unfamiliar, it is much harder to locate, and developing Windows software is already difficult enough. The really difficult bugs usually occur late on Friday when the project is behind schedule!

It is helpful if you try and use the debugger when learning Delphi, since it saves a lot of time and frustration in the long term.

12

Graphics

Introduction

Graphics can make the difference between an application that looks uninteresting and unclear and an application that users like and find works well. In this chapter you will learn about:

- Creating graphics at run-time and design-time.
- The **Canvas** property.
- Using the graphics controls.
- Using the graphics methods.
- Using panels and speed buttons.
- The **TColorDialog** component for changing pen and brush colours.

Creating Graphics

There are three ways of including graphics in your application:

- Create the graphics at design-time using the graphics controls.
- Add them at design-time.
- Add them at run-time.

This chapter covers each of these three aspects in turn.

The Graphics Controls

Fig. 12.1   *The **TShape** component is on the Additional page of the Component Palette*

Graphics can be created at design-time using the **TShape** component (fig. 12.1) which is on the Additional page of Component Palette (fig. 12.2).

The **TShape** component

Fig. 12.2   *The Additional page of the Component Palette*

The **Shape** property of this component (fig. 12.2) determines which of six basic shapes are drawn.

These shapes can be drawn at design-time (fig. 12.3). In addition they can be drawn at design-time using a corresponding set of methods. Methods are function calls that you use at run-time, for example, the **LineTo** method draws a line.

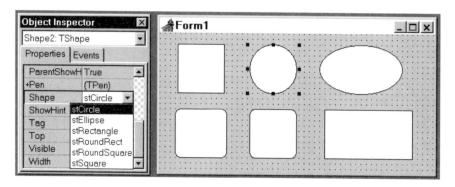

Fig. 12.3   *Drawing shapes at design-time*

The colours and styles of the shapes are dependent on the **Color** and **Style** of the Brush object.

Adding Graphics at Design-time

The sort of shapes you can add with the **TShape** component are very limited.

You can also add graphics at design time by using a **TImage** component (fig. 12.4).

   Fig. 12.4   *The **TImage** component is on the Additional page of the Component Palette*

The **TImage** component (fig. 12.5) defines an area of the form that can be used to contain an icon or bit-mapped image.

The **Picture** property of the component specifies the image that the component holds. If you click on the three dots adjacent to the **Picture** property of a **TImage**

The TImage component

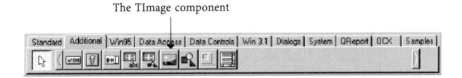

Fig. 12.5 *The TImage component*

component in the Object Inspector, the Picture Editor is displayed (fig. 12.6) and you can browse through the available icons or bit-mapped files, by first clicking on the *Load* button.

Fig. 12.6
The Picture Editor

When you have made your choice, you can choose **OK** and the picture appears in the **TImage** component – if you want to save the file you have chosen in a different place, select the **Save** option and specify the filename where you want to save it.

Using the Image Editor

Delphi provides a powerful image editor which can be found by selecting the **Image Editor** option (fig. 12.7) from the **Tools** menu.

- To open an existing file and to edit it, select the **Open** option from the **File** menu.
- When you have opened a file, you can edit it and save the modified version.

This allows you to edit existing images or to create new images.

The colours palette allows you to choose the foreground and background colours, and the fill pattern for those objects that can be filled. There is also a set of tools (fig. 12.8) which allows you to draw a standard set of outline or filled shapes, to add text and to select and move parts of the image.

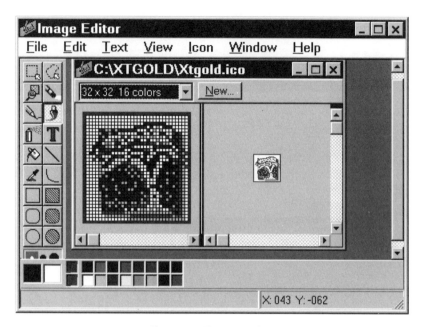

Fig. 12.7   *The Image Editor*

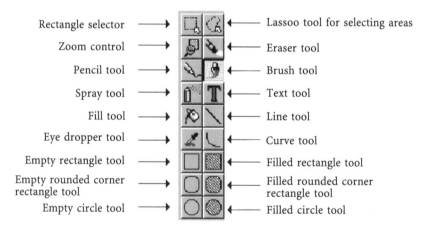

Rectangle selector ——→   ←—— Lassoo tool for selecting areas

Zoom control ——→   ←—— Eraser tool

Pencil tool ——→   ←—— Brush tool

Spray tool ——→   ←—— Text tool

Fill tool ——→   ←—— Line tool

Eye dropper tool ——→   ←—— Curve tool

Empty rectangle tool ——→   ←—— Filled rectangle tool

Empty rounded corner ——→   ←—— Filled rounded corner
rectangle tool   rectangle tool

Empty circle tool ——→   ←—— Filled circle tool

Fig. 12.8   *The Image Editor drawing tools*

Adding Graphics at Run-time

When you draw graphics at run-time, you draw onto the **Canvas** of an object. The **Canvas** is a property of the object and is in fact an object itself.

The four key properties of the **Canvas** object are:

- The pen, which is used for drawing lines
- The brush, which is used for filling in shapes
- The font, which describes the font of any text
- A pixel array, which represents the graphical image.

The Pen Property

The **Pen** property (fig. 12.9) controls the appearance of lines that are drawn on the canvas. In particular, you can control the following properties of the pen:

- **Color**
- **Width**
- **Style**
- **Mode.**

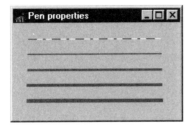

Fig. 12.9
The **Pen** property

The **Color** property is set using the **RGB** function. This specifies the red, green and blue components of the colour as three values between 0 and 255. If all of them are 0, the colour is black. If all are 255, the colour is white.

The **Width** is the width of the line drawn in pixels. The **Style** determines if the line is solid, dotted, or dashed. The **Mode** property allows you to specify the way in which the colour of the pen is combined with the colour of the canvas that is being drawn on.

Drawing Lines

A canvas can have two sorts of lines using the pen: straight lines and polylines. Straight lines are the shortest lines between two points. Polylines are a string of connected straight lines.

To draw straight lines use the **LineTo** method, which draws a line from the current point to the specified point. If you want to move the current point, use the **MoveTo** method.

The top left of the area is the (0,0) position, and the default units are pixels.

This code does draw five lines which gradually increase in thickness from top to bottom (fig. 12.9). Only the first line is dashed. The dashed style is ignored for the other lines. This is not a fault with Delphi; most video drivers do not support dashed lines greater than one pixel in width.

```
procedure TForm1.FormPaint(Sender: Tobject);
var
    count: integer;
begin
    Canvas.Pen.Style := psdashdot;
    Canvas.Pen.Color := RGB(120,120,200);

for count := 1 to 5 do
    begin
        Canvas.Pen.Width := count;
        Canvas.Moveto(20, count*20);
        Canvas.LineTo(200, count*20);
    end;
end;
```

The possible values for the **Style** property are **psSolid, psDash, psDot, psDashDot, psDashDotDot** and **psClear**.

You can draw directly on the form or alternatively you can create a **TImage** component and draw onto that using the **Canvas** properties of the image. If you want to draw a line directly onto a form, you specify:

form1.Canvas.LineTo(200,400); or Canvas.LineTo(200,400);

relying on defaults.

If you want to draw on an image called *image1* you specify

image1.Canvas.LineTo(200,200);

Ensure the co-ordinates that you specify for the line are within the co-ordinate frame of the specified drawing area, in this case either the form or the **TImage** component.

Drawing Shapes

Delphi has several methods that allow you to draw a range of shapes at run-time corresponding to the range of shapes that you can draw at design-time.

To draw a rectangle, use the **Rectangle** method (fig. 12.10). The parameters are the co-ordinates of the top left corner and the co-ordinates of the bottom right corner. To draw an ellipse, use the **Ellipse** method.

The code required to draw this image is:

Canvas.Rectangle(50,50,250,100);
Canvas.Ellipse(50,50,250,100);

The ellipse drawn is the largest ellipse that fits within the specified rectangle.

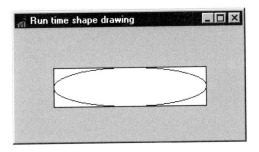

Fig. 12.10
*Using the **Rectangle** method*

To draw a round cornered rectangle, use the **RoundRect** method, specify the same four initial parameters as for the **Rectangle** method and, in addition, a further parameter that specifies the diameter of the quadrant that goes into the corner of the shape. For example:

Canvas.RoundRect(50,50,250,100,20);

draws a round cornered rectangle of the same size and position as the previous rectangle, but with a quarter circle of diameter 20 pixels in each corner.

In addition to these shapes, you can draw a range of other shapes using Delphi functions:

Function	Action
Arc	Draws an arc – a section of an ellipse.
Chord	Draws the chord of an arc.
FrameRect	Draws a frame around a rectangle.
Pie	Draws an arc and then draws lines to the centre.
Polygon	Draws a specified series of lines and joins the end of the last line to the start of the first.
PolyLine	Draws a specified series of lines but does close the shape.

The Brush Property

While the **Pen** property of a canvas determines the size and style of lines, the **Brush** property determines the way in which areas are filled.

The **Brush** has three properties:

- Color
- Style
- Bitmap.

The **Color** property gives the colour of filled shapes and areas. You can change this at run-time by assigning the colour using the **RGB** function.

If you want to draw a filled red ellipse, specify the **Color** property of the brush before drawing the ellipse.

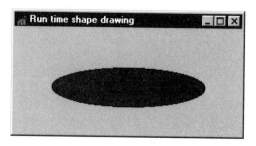

Fig. 12.11
The **Brush** property

The code required to draw the image in fig. 12.11 is:

Canvas.Brush.Color := RGB(255,0,0);
Canvas.Ellipse(50,50,250,100);

The **Style** property of the brush determines if the brush fills the ellipse with either solid colour, or lines. The available options for the **Style** property are: **bsSolid, bsClear, bsHorizontal, bsVertical, bsFDiagonal, bsBDiagional, bsCross** and **bsDiagCross**. Fig. 12.12 shows the ellipse filled with vertical (red) lines.

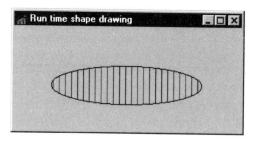

Fig. 12.12
The **Style** property

The code required to draw this image is:

Canvas.Brush.Color := RGB(255,0,0);
Canvas.Brush.Style := bsVertical
Canvas.Ellipse(50,50,250,100);

The Pixel Array

Any image is made up of a two-dimensional grid of pixels. You can both read and set the colour of individual pixels. To read the colour, you use the **Pixels** property of the canvas. For example:

form1.Font.Text := Pixels[200,300];

changes the colour of the text on the form to the colour of the pixel at position 200,300.

To set the colour of a pixel, assign the **Pixels** property to a value:

Canvas.Pixels[10,10] := RGB(20,30,200);

Creating a Drawing Application

One of the best ways to understand how these graphics features are used is to develop an application. This section develops a drawing package that allows you to create a set of shapes of different colours. The completed application is shown in fig. 12.13.

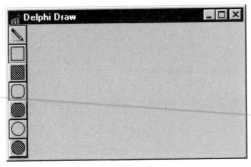

Fig. 12.13
A Delphi drawing program

The first stage is to create the tool bar. This is in fact a panel with a collection of speed bars on it.

Fig. 12.14   The **TPanel** *component is the last component on the right of the Standard page of the Component Palette*

This component can be positioned anywhere on the form, but in this case we want it to be aligned on the left of the form (fig. 12.14). The **Align** property needs to be assigned to **AlLeft**.

Each of the buttons on the panel are speed buttons (fig. 12.5).

Fig. 12.15   The **TSpeedButton** *component is on the Additional page of the Component Palette*

You need seven speed buttons aligned one on top of the other; the panel can be re-sized so that it cannot be seen underneath the speed buttons. One of the key properties of speed buttons is the **Glyph** property which is a bit map displayed on the face of the button. If you double click on this property for the speed button, the Picture Editor is displayed as shown in fig. 12.16.

Fig. 12.16
*Using the Picture Editor for setting the **Glyph** property*

This allows you to browse through your directories to find the image that you want on the face of your button. If you have used the default directories when installing Delphi, the bit maps that you need are in the DELPHI\DEMOS\DOC\-GRAPHEX directory.

SpeedButton Properties

When a speed button appears pressed, its **Down** property is true. To disable a button, set its **Enabled** property to false.

Another useful property is the **GroupIndex** property which allows a collection of speed buttons to act as one unit. If all the speed buttons have the same **GroupIndex** value, when one appears pressed, the others automatically appear not pressed.

Your design screen should look like fig. 12.13 when you run the program. So far the program does nothing, as the background code needs to be added.

When you click on one of the speed buttons, it simply selects the function that you are going to carry out, drawing a line, circle, round cornered square, or square. There are filled versions for the shapes. When you have selected a function, you then click the left mouse button to start the drawing. When you release the button, the drawing object is complete. If, for example, you select the speed button for drawing a square, one corner is given by the position where you press the mouse button, and the diagonally opposite corner where you release the button.

Writing the Event Handlers

To select the function, you need to put some code in each of the **OnClick** event handlers for the speed buttons. The variable *Tool* is assigned a different value depending on which button is pressed. Rather than using a different number to represent each function, *Tool* can be defined as an enumerated type, so that a name is assigned to each state. In the variable declaration section of the form you need to add these lines of code:

```
Type TTool : (Line,
              Rect, Filled_Rect,
              Round_Rect, Filled_Round_Rect,
              Ellip, Filled_Ellip);
```

This declares a new type. If a variable of type *TTool* is defined by:

```
Tool : TTool;
```

you can assign any of the enumerated values to the *Tool* variable. For example:

```
Tool := Filled_Ellip;
```

The event handler for the speed button that draws outline rectangles becomes:

```
procedure TForm1.SpeedButton2Click(Sender: TObject);
begin
      Tool := Rect;
      form1.Canvas.Brush.Style := bsClear;
end;
```

The brush **Style** property is set to **bsClear**, which ensures that the rectangle drawn is an outline and not filled. Similarly in the **OnClick** event handler for the filled rectangle:

```
procedure TForm1.SpeedButton3Click(Sender: TObject);
begin
      Tool := Filled_Rect;
      form1.Canvas.Brush.Style := bsSolid;
end;
```

The **OnClick** event handlers for the other speed buttons are modified in the same way. If the shape is not filled, the **Brush.Style** property is assigned to **bsClear**. The line drawing tool does not require the **Brush.Style** property of the canvas to be changed.

In the **OnMouseDown** event handler for the form, the current position of the mouse needs to be saved, since this is used as the starting point for the shape or line, but it is not until the **OnMouseUp** event that the shape is drawn. You need this code in the **OnMouseDown** handler for the form:

```
procedure TForm1.FormMouseDown(Sender: TObject;
Button: MouseButton;
   Shift: TShiftState; X, Y: Integer);
begin
      startx := x;
      starty := y;
      form1.Canvas.MoveTo(x, y);
end;
```

The integer variables *startx* and *starty* are defined in the **var** section of the form. The **OnMouseDown** handler saves current x and y co-ordinates of the mouse and moves the cursor to that point using the **MoveTo** method.

In the **OnMouseUp** handler for the form, different action is taken depending on the shape selected, as indicated by the value of the *Tool* variable.

```
procedure TForm1.FormMouseUp(Sender: TObject; Button: TMouseButton;
   Shift: TShiftState; X, Y: Integer);
begin
case Tool of
      line: form1.Canvas.LineTo(x, y);
```

```
Rect, Filled_Rect: form1.Canvas.Rectangle(startx, starty, x, y);
Round_Rect,Filled_Round_Rect:
    form1.Canvas.Roundrect(startx, starty, x, y);
Ellip, Filled_Ellip : form1.Canvas.Ellipse(startx, starty, x, y);
end;
end;
```

The drawing package now works as shown in fig. 12.17, producing both outline and filled shapes.

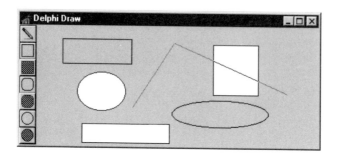

Fig. 12.17
The drawing package

Rubber Banding

This is not a very sophisticated system. The most noticeable aspect is that when you drag the mouse, you do not see the shape that you are drawing with the start position anchored and with the opposite corner moving as the mouse moves. The effect is called rubber banding, and to achieve this the **OnMouseMove** event needs to be changed. When the mouse is moved, the previous shape is erased and a new one drawn with its corner at the new mouse position. The new **OnMouseMove** event handler now looks like this:

```
procedure TForm1.FormMouseMove(Sender: TObject; Shift: TShiftState; X,
    Y: Integer);
begin
    if (drawing = true) then
    begin
    Canvas.Pen.Mode := pmNotXor;
        case Tool of
        Rect : begin
                Canvas.Rectangle(startx, starty, previousx, previousy);
                Canvas.Rectangle(startx, starty, x, y);
                end;
        Round_Rect : begin
                Canvas.Roundrect(startx, starty, previousx, previousy);
                Canvas.Roundrect(startx, starty, x, y);
                end;
```

```
            Ellip : begin
                     Canvas.Ellipse(startx, starty, previousx, previousy);
                     Canvas.Ellipse(startx, starty, x, y);
                     end;
            Line : begin
                     Canvas.Moveto(startx, starty);
                     Canvas.LineTo(previousx, previousy);
                     Canvas.MoveTo(startx, starty);
                     Canvas.LineTo(x, y);
                     end;
          end;
       previousx := x;
       previousy := y;
       end;
  Canvas.Pen.Mode := pmCopy;
  end;
```

The mode of the pen for the canvas is set to **pmNotXor** at the start of the procedure. If a drawing is in progress (the *drawing* boolean is set to true in the **OnMouseDown** event and to false in the **OnMouseUp** event), the first action is to erase the previous shape drawn and to draw a new shape. The old shape is overwritten, and the effect of the pen mode of **pmNotXor** is to erase a line if a new line is drawn over it. If no line is present at the place where a new line is drawn, the new line is shown. As the mouse is dragged, a different shape is drawn for each of the shapes available, showing what would be drawn if the mouse button was released at that point.

The Line tool is a little different. The **LineTo** method draws a line from the previous position to a new one. Therefore, the **MoveTo** method has to be used to reposition the cursor to the starting point and the **LineTo** method is used to erase the old line. Next, the **MoveTo** method is used to move back to the starting position and then the **LineTo** method draws the line to the new position.

At the end of the procedure the current position of the cursor is saved in *previousx* and *previousy*, and this is used the next time the procedure is called (that is, the next time the mouse moves) to erase the previous line or shape. Finally, the pen mode is returned to **pmCopy**.

Using the ColorDialog

The application is rather dull when working just in black and white, but there is a wide range of ways of introducing colour. The colour of the lines drawn is controlled by the **Color** property of the pen, while the colour of the filled shapes is determined by the color property of the brush.

The easiest way of doing this is to use the **TColorDialog** component (fig. 12.18).

Fig. 12.18   *The **TColorDialog** component is on the Dialogs page of the Component Palette*

- First change the layout of the speed buttons, to improve its appearance and to allow the addition of two ordinary buttons which run the **TColorDialog** component. The completed running application is shown in fig. 12.20.
- Change the **Align** property of the panel to **AlTop**; this moves the panel to the top of the form. You need to move the speed buttons to new positions.
- Add the **TColorDialog** component to the form – this is not visible at run-time, so it does not matter where it is placed.
- Next create two ordinary buttons with the captions *Pen Colour* and *Brush Colour*. In the **OnClick** event handler for the *Pen Colour* button, insert the code:

*colordialog1.**Execute**;*

- When this button is clicked, the **Execute** method of the **TColorDialog** dialog (fig. 12.19) is executed and the color dialog is displayed.

Fig. 12.19
*The **TColorDialog***

When you click on a colour to select it and then click on **OK**, the **Color** property of the **TColorDialog** is assigned. To change the colour of the pen, the following line must be added after the **Execute** method:

*form1.**Canvas.Pen.Color** := colordialog1.**Color**;*

Similarly, the click event handler for the *Brush Colour* button is:

*colordialog1.**Execute**;*
*form1.**Canvas.Brush.Color** := colordialog1.**Color**;*

This time the brush colour is assigned. The final version of the program is shown in fig. 12.20.

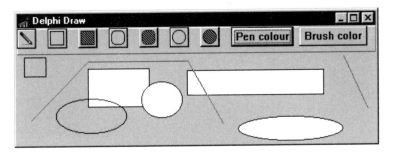

Fig. 12.20   *The Delphi drawing program*

Using the Clipboard

The Windows Clipboard is a useful way of exchanging graphical information between applications. It is straightforward in Delphi both to read from the clipboard and to put images into it.

To copy information into the clipboard, use the **Assign** method. For example, to copy the image in a **Timage** components called *MyImage* to the clipboard:

Clipboard.Assign(MyImage.Picture);

If you want to paste an image from the clipboard into an image, first check that the contents of the clipboard is a bit-map. The **HasFormat** method does this. This method is passed a data type and it returns true if that type of data is held in the clipboard. To check for a bit-mapped image:

If Clipboard.HasFormat(CF_BITMAP) then ...
{ if true is returned, the contents is a bit-map }

A bit-map can be created using the **Create** method and the contents of the clipboard can then be copied to it:

MyBitmap := TBitmap.Create;
MyImage.Canvas.Draw(0, 0, MyBitmap);

If you want to delete *MyBitmap* after using it, you can do this with the **Free** method:

MyBitMap.Free

13

Mouse and Keyboard Events

Introduction

Mouse and keyboard events are crucial to many Windows applications. This chapter looks at mouse events. In this chapter you will learn about:

- The mouse events.
- The keyboard events.

The Mouse Events

In Delphi there are three mouse events:

- OnMouseUp.
- OnMouseDown.
- OnMouseMove.

Whenever one of these mouse events occurs, Delphi goes to the appropriate event handler and passes five parameters:

Parameter	Meaning
Sender	The object that detects the mouse event.
Button	Indicates if the left, right, or middle button was used (*mbLeft, mbRight, mbMiddle*).
Shift	Gives the state of the **Alt**, **Ctrl** and **Shift** keys at the time of the event.
X	The X co-ordinate of the mouse position.
Y	The Y co-ordinate of the mouse position.

The same event handler is called, irrespective of which mouse button is clicked – if you need to distinguish between them, you have to check the value of the *Button* parameter in the event handler.

The Scribble Program

The scribble program (fig. 13.1) tracks the movement of the mouse on the screen. This is typical of applications that take a few lines to write in Delphi and yet are very difficult to write in most other programming environments.

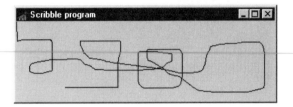

Fig. 13.1
The scribble program

- Create a new project.
- Change the **Caption** property of the form to *Scribble program*.
- View the Events page of the Object Inspector, double click on the **OnMouseMove** event and enter the following line of code:

  Canvas.LineTo(X, Y);

The **LineTo** method draws a line from the previous position to the current position.

OnMouseDown and OnMouseUp Events

The **OnMouseDown** and **OnMouseUp** events occur when a mouse button is pressed and released. A variation of the scribble program is to draw a line from the previous mouse position to a new mouse position when a mouse button is pressed (fig. 13.2).

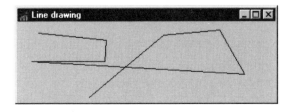

Fig. 13.2
The continuous line drawing program

- Create a new project.
- Change the **Caption** property of the form to *Line Drawing*.

- View the Events page of the Object Inspector, double click on the **OnMouse-Up** event and enter the following line of code:

Canvas.LineTo(X, Y);

This program can only join a single connected line. In order to draw separate lines (fig. 13.3), the **OnMouseDown** event handler needs to be changed to include the line:

Canvas.MoveTo(X, Y);

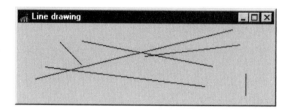

Fig. 13.3
The line drawing program

When the mouse button is pressed, the current X, Y position of the mouse is moved to that position. If the mouse is moved with the button pressed and then released, the **OnMouseUp** event will draw a line from the position where the mouse button is pressed to the position where it is released.

The Keyboard Events

Delphi has three keyboard events:

- **OnKeyDown**
- **OnKeyPress**
- **OnKeyUp**.

These occur in the following order, for example, when **Shift+A** is pressed:

- **OnKeyDown** (Shift)
- **OnKeyDown** (Shift A)
- **OnKeyPress** (A)
- **OnKeyUp** (Shift A)
- **OnKeyUp**.

Every time that a key is pressed, the **OnKeyDown** and the **OnKeyUp** events are generated. However, the **OnKeyPress** event only occurs when a key that has a valid ASCII code is pressed. Alphanumeric characters, for example, produce the **OnKeyPress** event.

When a combination of keys is pressed, for example, **Shift+A**, or **Ctrl+C**, the **OnKeyDown** event passes the value of the previous key pressed down to the next

OnKeyDown event, so that this event is aware that a pair of keys has been pressed.

The **OnKeyUp** event only has the value of the last key combination pressed.

The **OnKeyPress** event is not created by the **Ctrl** or **Shift** keys, and in the example it responds to the pressing of the *"A"* key. An important distinction between these events is that while the **OnKeyPress** event differentiates between *"a"* and *"A"*, **OnKeyUp** and **OnKeyDown** are not aware of the difference between lower case and upper case letters.

If you want an event handler that responds to non-ASCII characters such as Page Up and Insert, you need to use the **OnKeyUp** or **OnKeyDown** event handlers.

Using the **OnKeyPress** event (fig. 13.4), this application displays a small bitmap of a car on a form and moves it to the left or right depending on whether you press *"R"* or *"r"* for right and *"L"* or *"l"* for left.

Fig. 13.4
*The **OnKeyPress** event*

- Start a new project.
- Set the **KeyPreview** property of the form to true.

The **KeyPreview** ensures that all keyboard events can be handled at the form level, rather than by writing an event handler for each component on the form.

- Create an **TImage** component (fig. 13.5). This is found on the additional page of the component toolbar.

   *Fig. 13.5   The **TImage** component*

- To load the picture at run-time when the form is activated, you have to change the event handler for the **OnActivate** event. It should look like this:

```
procedure TForm1.FormActivate(Sender: TObject);
begin
    image1.Picture.LoadFromFile('c:\windows\cars.bmp');
end;
```

- To move the car to the right or left in response to the keyboard events, the following two lines of indented code must be added to the **OnKeyPress** event handler for the form:

```
procedure TForm1.FormKeyPress(Sender: TObject; var Key: Char);
begin
    if (key = 'L') or (key = 'l') then image1.left := image1.left - 10;
    if (key = 'R') or (key = 'r') then image1.left := image1.left + 10;
end;
```

The **left** property of the image determines its position relative to the left of the form. Since the **OnKeyPress** event distinguishes between upper and lower case letters, you must test for both.

Using the OnKeyUp and OnKeyDown Events

In order to use the arrowed keys to move the car up, down, left and right, you have to use the **OnKeyUp** or the **OnKeyDown** event handlers.

- Delete the event handle for the **OnKeyPress** event.
- Add the following code to the **OnKeyDown** event handler:

```
procedure TForm1.FormKeyDown(Sender: TObject; var Key: Word
    Shift: TShiftState);
begin
if (key = vk_right) then image1.left := image1.left + 10;
if (key = vk_left) then image1.left := image1.left - 10;
if (key = vk_up) then image1.top := image1.top - 10;
if (key = vk_down) then image1.top := image1.top + 10;
end;
```

The **Top** property of the image determines its position relative to the top of the form. This event handler is called when any key event occurs, including the arrowed keys. These keys have symbolic or virtual key codes. The code for the right arrow key is **vk_right**, for the down arrow **vk_down**. An exhaustive list is given in the Delphi Help under the topic *Virtual key codes*.

14

Using Databases

Introduction

One of the most important features of Delphi is that it allows you quickly to develop database application for a wide range of standard databases including Paradox, dBase and most SQL database packages. It has a powerful tool called the Database Forms Expert which allows you to browse through and amend databases very rapidly. If you want complete flexibility in developing your application, Delphi offers a wide range of database components that allow you to specify exactly what you want. In this chapter you will learn about:

- Databases.
- Data controls.
- Reading and updating databases.

What is a Database?

Before we look at how Delphi deals with databases, it is useful to have a brief look at what a database is.

All the information in a database is stored in tables like that shown in fig. 14.1.

Each table is made up of rows and columns. A row contains a collection of information about one object; in this case, each row contains four pieces of information about different countries. Another name for a row is a record.

Every column has the same type of information about all the different objects, for example, the *Country* column contain the names of all the countries.

Records can be read from the database one at a time; the record that is the focus of attention is called the current record, even though many records may be displayed.

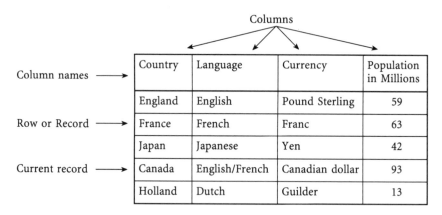

Fig. 14.1   *Database terminology*

The way in which different databases store their information varies enormously. Some use a collection of files while others use a single file but, from the user's point of view, the basic structure is the same:

- The complete set of data is called the database.
- The data is separated into one or more tables.
- The data in each table is stored in a set of rows and columns.
- Each piece of data is called a field.

The data in each record can be of different types, in this case the Country, Language and Currency are text fields while the population is an integer field. Other data types such as bitmaps and currency can also be stored.

What Databases Can Delphi Use

When you install Delphi, it is configured to allow access to three databases:

- Paradox
- dBase
- SQL databases.

If you are creating large database applications you need to use the Client/Server version of Delphi 2.0. The applications developed in this chapter can be done with the Desktop version.

The Database Forms Expert

Delphi allows you great flexibility in using databases, but it also provides a quick way of creating a database browser which allows you to view individual records, move through each records in the database, and add and delete records.

This example uses the Form Expert to create a browser for viewing an animals database, which is supplied with Delphi. To create the browser, select the **Form Expert** option (fig. 14.2) from the **Database** menu.

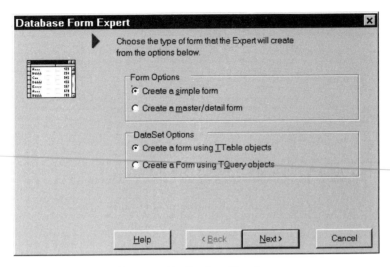

Fig. 14.2   *The Database Form Expert*

Select the **Create a simple form** option and the **Create a form using TTable objects,** and click on **Next.**

The database that you are going to open is called *animals.dbf* and is usually stored in the c:\delphi\demos\data directory (fig. 14.3), although this may be different if you have specified different directories during installation.

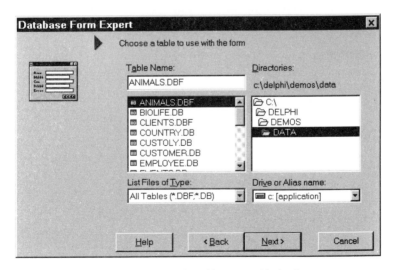

Fig. 14.3   *Choosing the table to use with the form*

Select this database and click on **Next**. You have now specified the database that you want to browse. The next stage is to specify the fields of the database that you want to display (fig. 14.4).

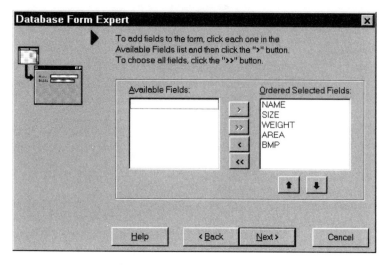

Fig. 14.4   *Adding fields to the form*

These can be selected one at a time by clicking on the button with the left-pointing arrow, or you can select all of them by clicking on the double arrow. After selecting all of the fields, click on **Next**.

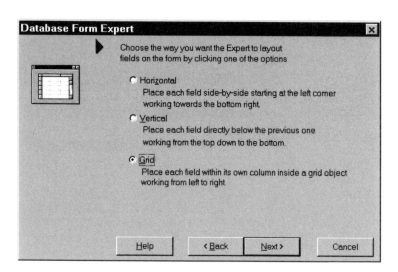

Fig. 14.5   *Choosing the form layout*

The final stage is to say how you want the data to be displayed on your browser form (fig. 14.5). In this case, select the **Grid** option and click on **Next**.

Click on the **Create** option on the final menu and you have created the browser program. The form that you have produced looks like the one shown in fig. 14.6.

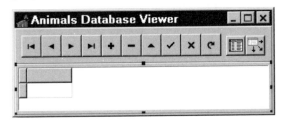

Fig. 14.6
The completed animals database viewer

Running the Browser

When you have compiled and linked the program (just press **F9**) you are ready to run it. The running program is shown in fig. 14.7.

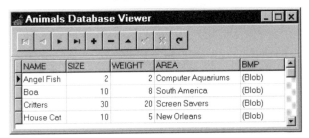

Fig. 14.7
Running the animals database

The browser allows you to move through the database and to amend, add and delete records, by using the toolbar.

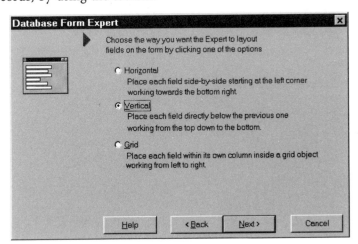

Fig. 14.8 *Choosing a vertical layout of fields on the form*

One of the problems with the present system is that the images of the animals are not displayed. If you want to see these images you need to display one record at a time. Specify that you want the fields of each record to be displayed one below the other – one record at a time. You can do this by selecting the **Vertical** option from the design screen, as shown in fig. 14.8, on the previous page.

The completed form in the design phase is shown in fig. 14.9.

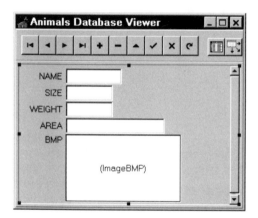

Fig. 14.9
The completed animals database

At this stage you can move any of the components, re-size them, or add additional ones in the usual way. When the program is run, it displays one record at a time including the image (fig. 14.10).

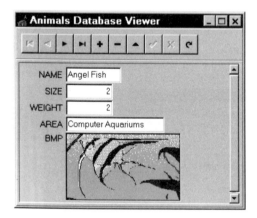

Fig. 14.10
The running animals database

Using Data Controls

The Database Form Expert provides a quick way of developing database applications, but sometimes you may want greater control over the way in which the data is transferred between your application and the database. Delphi provides a powerful set of controls for doing this.

If you select the Data Controls page of the Component Palette, you see a set of components that are similar to some components we have already looked at, for example, the image box (**TDBImage**), the list box **TDBList**, and so on. The difference is that the components on this page are data aware; that is, they can be connected to a field in the database. When the current record changes, the data aware component is updated.

The DataField Property

If you select the edit box used to store the name of the animal and view its properties in the Object Inspector, one of the properties is the **DataField** (fig. 14.11).

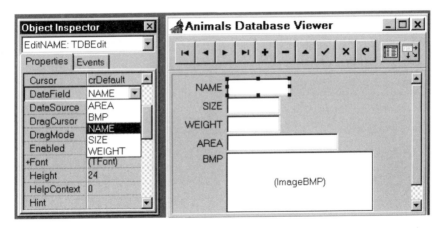

Fig. 14.11   *The DataField property*

In the case of this edit box the **DataField** property is *Name*; that is, the *Name* field in the database. If you click on the three dots adjacent to *Name*, you see a list of all the possible fields that can be assigned to this data aware edit box. If you do the same for the data aware components, you see that each has been assigned to a database field.

The DataSource Property

While the **DataField** property connects a component to a field in the database, the **DataSource** property of data aware components connects the component to a **TDataSource** component, which in turn specifies the database where the data is stored.

The TDataSource Component

Fig. 14.12   The ***TDataSource*** *component is on the Data Access page of the Component Palette*

The **TDateSource** component (fig. 14.12) can be seen on the form produced by the Database Forms Expert, shown in fig. 14.13 alongside the **TTable** component which you look at next.

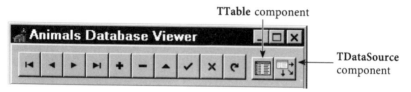

Fig. 14.13   *The **TTable** and **TDataSource** components*

If you look at the properties of this component in the Object Inspector (fig. 14.14), you see that it has very few:

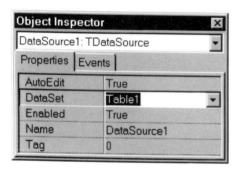

Fig. 14.14
*The **Dataset** property of the **TDataSource** component*

The **DataSet** property of this component is the key property. This property links the data aware components to the underlying database. The **DataSet** property specifies the name of the component that provides the data to the data aware components. This component can either be a **TTable** component or the **TQuery** component.

The TTable Component

Fig. 14.15   *The **TTable** component is on the Data Access page of the Component Palette*

This component (fig. 14.15) provides access to the database using the Borland Database Engine (BDE). In the animals database, the **TTable** component is used (fig. 14.16).

When you open the table, the **Active** property of the component is set to true.

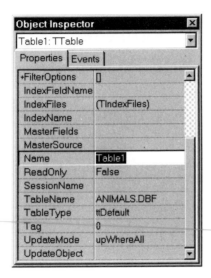

Fig. 14.16
*The properties of the **TTable** component*

The **DatabaseName** property contains the name of the database to be accessed and the **TableName** property specifies the table to be accessed. If you want to change either of these two properties, the **Active** property must be set to true.

The **ReadOnly** property must be false if you want to change the contents of the table. The **Exclusive** property must be true if you do not want any other application to have access to the table when you are using it.

The **TableType** property specifies the format of the database table, such as dBase or Paradox.

The TQuery Component

Fig. 14.17 *The **TQuery** component is on the Data Access page of the Component Palette.*

The **TQuery** component (fig. 14.17) behaves in a similar way to the **TTable** except that it allows Delphi applications to issue SQL commands to the database. Most of the properties are the same as properties of the **TTable** component.

The **DatabaseName** property specifies the database used for the query, while the SQL property contains the SQL statement used to recover the data.

To see how this is used you are going to return to the Form Expert to create an application, but this time you are going to specify in the **DataSet option** that you want to create a form using the **TQuery** object, as shown in fig. 14.18.

Next specify the biolife database (fig. 14.19), which is supplied as a part of Delphi.

Select all the available fields in the next screen. Choose a vertical alignment of fields, then create the application and run. The application looks like (fig. 14.20) when it runs.

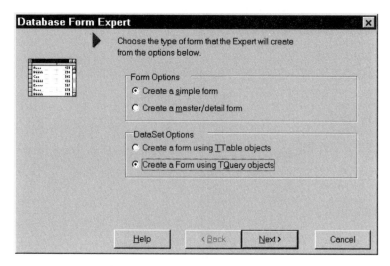

Fig. 14.18   *Using the **TQuery** component*

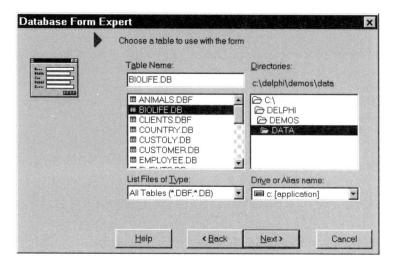

Fig. 14.19   *Selecting the biofile database*

If you return to the design screen and select the **TQuery** component, you can see its properties in the Object Inspector (fig. 14.21).

The most surprising thing is that both the **DatabaseName** and the **DataSource** properties are blank. This is because this information is included in the SQL property. Select this property and double click on it to display the string list editor (fig. 14.22).

The full name of the database, the table and the data fields to be read are given in the SQL.

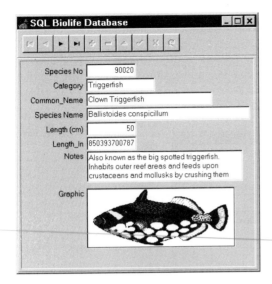

Fig. 14.20
Running the SQL biolife database

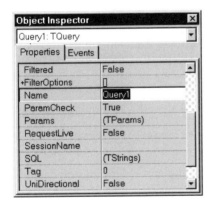

Fig. 14.21
*The properties of the **TQuery** component*

Fig. 14.22
*SQL for the **TQuery** component*

Creating a Database Application

Database applications can be readily created without using the Database Forms Expert. This section looks at creating an application to read from a database which is supplied with Delphi.

The final design screen should look like this:

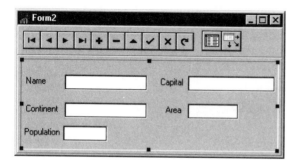

Fig. 14.23
The completed countries database

- Create a new form by clicking on the **New Form** option from the **File** menu. Specify a blank form.
- Create a panel at the top of the screen for the data controls. The **TPanel** component is at the end of the Standard page of the Component Palette.
- Add the **TDataSource** and the **TTable** components from the Data Controls page of the Component Palette.
- Next you need to add a new component called the **TDBNavigator** (fig. 14.25)

 Fig. 14.24   The **TDBNavigator** *component is on the Data Controls page of the Component Palette*

This provides a range of controls for viewing and amending the database (fig. 14.25).

 **Fig. 14.25**   The **TDBNavigator** *component*

These buttons in the **TDBNavigator** component have the following meanings:

Button	Description
First	Sets the current record to the first record.
Previous	Moves to the previous record (if not already at the start).
Next	Moves to the next record (if not already at the end).
Last	Moves to the last record.
Insert	Inserts a new record.
Delete	Deletes the current record.
Edit	Allows the current record to be edited.
Post	Writes changes in the current record to the database.
Cancel	Cancels the edits made to the current record.
Refresh	Updates the display of the current record.

The next stage in our database application is to add a **TScrollBox** component (fig. 14.26).

 Fig. 14.26   *The **TScrollBox** component is on the Additional page of the Component Palette*

The scroll box acts as a container for the five data fields.

All the components are now set up, but the links to the database have to be constructed.

- For the name edit box, assign the **DataField** property to *Name* (if you click on the three dots on the right of the field, all the possible fields are displayed). Assign the **DataSource** property to *DataSource1*, the default name of the **TDataSource** component.
- Repeat this for all the other edit boxes, assigning the **DataSource** of all to *DataSource1* and the appropriate value to the **FieldName** property.
- Assign the **DataSet** property of the **TDataSource** component to *Table1*, the default name of the **TTable** component.
- Finally, specify the **DatabaseName** property for the **TTable** component, in this case it is *c:\delphi\demo\data*, and set the **TableName** property to *country.dbf*.

This completes the database application and it is ready to run.

Fig. 14.27
The running countries database

When the program is run, it displays the details of one country at a time (fig. 14.27).

15

Delphi Components Reference

Introduction

So far we have looked at some Delphi components but there are a great deal more. This chapter gives a summary of both components that we have already looked, as well as some new ones.

If you want to get the excellent context-sensitive Help on any of the components, select the component on the Component Palette and press **F1**.

The Standard Page

 The **TMainMenu** component creates a menu bar and the associated drop-down menus.

 The **TPopUpMenu** component creates a pop-up menu. This menu is available when you click the right mouse button.

 The **TLabel** component displays a small amount of text on a form. The text is held in the **Caption** property. If you change the text, the label can automatically re-size if the **AutoSize** property is set to true.

If you do not want the background of the label to hide the background, set the **Transparent** property (fig. 15.1) to true.

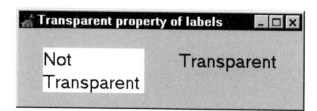

Fig. 15.1
*The **Transparent** property*

The **TEdit** component displays a single line of text and allows the user to edit it.

The **Modified** property is set to true if the text is changed. If you do not want to be able to change text, set the **ReadOnly** property to true.

The **AutoSelect** property automatically selects the text when the component has the focus.

A useful property is the **PassWordChar** property (fig. 15.2). Setting this to a particular character means that Delphi only displays that character when typing into the box.

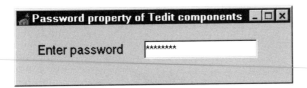

Fig. 15.2
*The **Password** property*

 The **TMemo** component displays text and allows the user to enter text. It is similar in operation to the **TEdit** component except that multiple lines can be entered and displayed.

You can add scrollbars if you set the **ScrollBars** property, setting the property to **Horizontal, Vertical,** or **Both.**

Most of the properties of the **TMemo** component are the same as the properties of the **TEdit** component. The **Lines** property of the **TMemo** component, however, is not found in the **TEdit** component. This property allows you to add, delete, insert and move lines using the **Add, Insert** and **Delete** methods. For example:

*MyMemo.**Lines.Add**('This instruction adds another line');*

 The **TButton** component. A default button is one that executes an **OnClick** event when return is pressed. A cancel button is one whose **OnClick** event is executed when **Escape** is pressed.

 The **TCheckBox** component. This component gives the user the choice of choosing an option. When the box is selected, the **Checked** property changes and an **OnClick** event occurs.

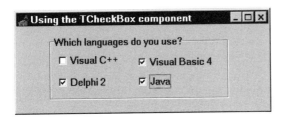

Fig. 15.3
Using check boxes

You can select any number of check boxes, unlike a group of radio buttons. The check boxes shown in fig. 15.3 are on a **TGroupBox** component.

The **TRadioButton** component is used to give the user the option of choosing one of a mutually exclusive set of options. If one radio button is selected, the other radio buttons in the group are automatically dese-lected. When a radio button is selected, the **Checked** property changes and an **OnClick** event occurs. Groups of radio buttons need to be placed within a container such as a group box. An example of radio buttons in a group box is shown in fig. 15.7.

The **TListBox** component is used to display a list of items (fig. 15.4). If the number of items in the list cannot all be shown in the box at the same time, a vertical scroll bar is added.

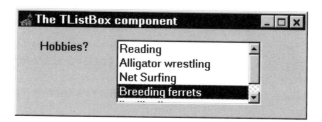

Fig. 15.4
Using list boxes

The items in the list are specified in the **Items** property. The **ItemIndex** property indicates which entry is selected. If you want the user to be able to select more than one item at a time, set the **MultiSelect** property to true. To determine if an item is selected, check the **Selected** and **SelCount** properties.

You can add, insert and delete items using the **Add, Delete** and **Insert** methods.

The **TComboBox** component (fig. 15.5). This behaves in the same way as a list box except that its appearance is different.

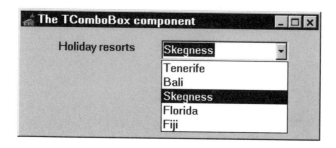

Fig. 15.5
Using combo boxes

You can select one of a list items from a drop-down list. You can change the style of a combo box by changing the **Style** property.

- **csDropDown**: this is a drop down list;
- **csSimple**: the list box part is always visible.
- **csDropDownList**: there is no edit box.
- **csOwnerDrawFixed**: each item has a height given by **ItemHeight**.
- **csOwnerDrawVariable**: each item can be of variable height.

 The **TScrollbar** component is used to scroll through information (fig. 15.6). The **Kind** property determines whether the scroll bars are horizontal or vertical. The **LargeChange** property determines how far you move through the data when you click on the scroll bar on the other side of the thumb tabs.

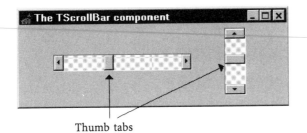

Fig. 15.6
Using scroll bars

Thumb tabs

The **SmallChange** property controls how far you move when you click on the arrows at the end of the scroll bar. The **Min** and **Max** properties determine how many positions are available.

 The **TGroupBox** component (fig. 15.7). This is a container component, which groups related components together on a form. The most common components grouped together are the radio buttons. Only one of a group of these buttons can be selected at any one time.

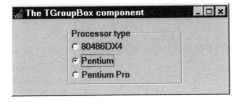

Fig. 15.7
*The **TGroupBox** component*

When the **TGroupBox** component is moved, all the components within it also move.

 The **TRadioGroup** component is a variant of the **TGroupBox** component designed for radio buttons. This component functions as a **TGroupBox** component with **TRadioButton** components on it. Rather than selecting a group box and then adding radio buttons separately, select the **Items** property and double click on it to enter the string editor. Every line you type corresponds to a radio button. The value of the **ItemIndex** property determines which radio button is selected.

 The **TPanel** component (fig. 15.8) is used to place panels on a form on which other components can be placed. Panels can be aligned with a form using the **Align** property, which ensures that the panel retains its position relative to the form.

The main use of panels is as containers for creating a tool bar or tool palette. Panels can be used as status bars in programs. To make panels stand out, you can change their appearance using the **BevelInner**, **BevelOuter**, **BevelWidth** and **BorderWidth** properties.

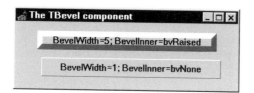

Fig. 15.8
The **TPanel** component

The Additional Page

 The **TBitBtn** component (fig. 15.9) behaves in the same way as an ordinary button, except that you can include a bit-map, sometimes called a glyph, on the button face. The **Kind** property specifies the bit-map to be displayed; alternatively, you can set it to **bkCustom**, in which case you specify your own bit-map.

Fig. 15.9
The **TBitBtn**
component

Help, Retry and Ignore are a few of the standard set of buttons.

In addition to a glyph, bit-map buttons have a **Caption** property like ordinary buttons, which specifies the text on the button.

 The **TSpeedButton** component are **TButton** components that have graphical images on their faces. Speed buttons are usually used with panels to create toolbars and tool palettes.

Speed buttons do not have a **Caption** property but can have up to four images associated with them, depending on the state of the button. The four images are used from left to right depending on the possible four states:

Up: unselected button state.
Disabled: grey image indicating that the button is not available.
Down: the button is pressed.
StayDown: the state when the button is pressed and remains pressed.

The images must all be the same size and contained in the same bit-map.

A useful property of speed buttons is the **GroupIndex** property. If the button has an index of zero, the button is pressed when the user clicks on it and pops up when the mouse button is released. If the **GroupIndex** is not zero, the mouse button stays down when pressed but any other button with the same **GroupIndex** that is down, pops up. This ensures that only one of a group of buttons is selected. The **Down** property can be set at design-time, and can be used to select a button when the program first runs.

 The **TMaskEdit** component behaves in the same way as an ordinary edit box, except that you can limit the characters that the user can enter by using the **EditMask** property. If you click on this property, the Mask Editor is displayed (fig. 15.10). This allows you to select one of a standard set of masks or to create your own.

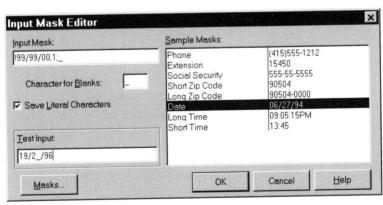

Fig. 15.10   *The Input Mask editor*

There are different sample masks available for different countries. You can change countries by selecting the **Masks** button.

The **TStringGrid** component behaves in the same way as an ordinary TDrawGrid component, but you are limited to using strings in the cells.

The **TDrawGrid** component allows you to display either textual or graphical information in a table. You can tell which cell is selected by looking at the **Selection** property. Cells can be filled at run-time using the **OnDrawCell** event. It is often necessary to know which cell the mouse is over, and you determine this using the **MouseToCell** method which returns the column and row co-ordinates of the cell that the mouse is in.

The **TImage** component is used to display a graphical image on a form. The **Picture** property specifies the image. If you want the image to re-size to fit the component, set the **Stretch** property (fig. 15.11) to true.

Fig. 15.11   *The **Stretch** property of the **TImage** component*

If you want the image to re-size to fill the image control, set the **AutoSize** property to true.

The **TShape** component (fig. 15.12) is used to add simple shapes to your forms.

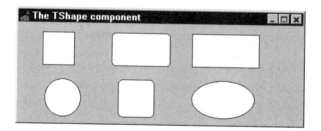

Fig. 15.12
*The **TShape** component*

The **Shape** property (fig. 15.12) determines which of the six shapes shown are displayed. One use of this control is to produce background shadows (fig. 15.13).

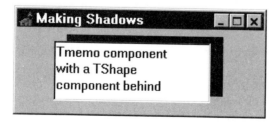

Fig. 15.13
*Using the **TShape** component to make shadows*

The **TBevel** component (fig. 15.14) puts bevelled lines, boxes and frames on a form. You choose which of these you want by using the **Shape** property.

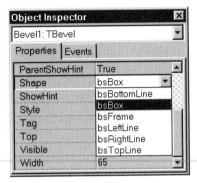

Fig. 15.14
*The **TBevel** component properties*

The **Shape** property determines whether the component is a box or a line. Four examples of how this component can appear are shown in fig. 15.15.

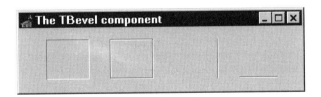

Fig. 15.15
*The **TBevel** component*

You control whether the bevel is raised or lowered depending on the **Style** property. This component is for display purposes only.

 The **TScrollBox** component (fig. 15.16) is a container that contains a scrollable area.

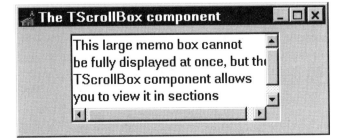

Fig. 15.16   *The **TScrollBox** component*

In this case, since all of the group of radio buttons do not fit into the scroll box, a vertical scroll bar is added. If required, a horizontal scroll bar is added to allow you to view the entire area within the box.

The Win 3.1 Page

  The **TDBLookupList** and the **TDBLookupCombo** components are only provided for backward compatibility. The **TDBLookupListBox** and the **TDBLookupComboBox** components should be used instead in Windows 95 applications.

The **TTabSet** component is used to display tabs, usually at the bottom of the **TNoteBook** component. The **Tabs** property contains the text that is displayed on each of the tabs.

 The **TOutline** component (fig. 15.17) is used for displaying multi-level hierarchical data.

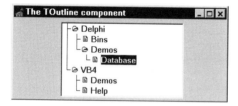

Fig. 15.17
*The **TOutline** component*

The data displayed is in the **Lines** property. Clicking on this invokes the String List Editor (fig. 15.18), where the data can be typed.

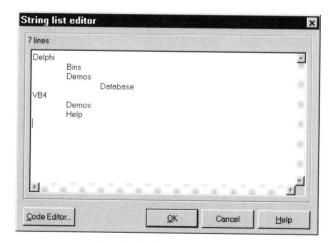

Fig. 15.18   *The string list editor*

The items in the hierarchy can be accessed by the **Items** property. The first item is referred to by **Items[1]**. You can add items using the **Add** method and replace existing items by using the **Insert** method.

Figure 15.19 gives a set of images adjacent to the text, which change when an item is selected.

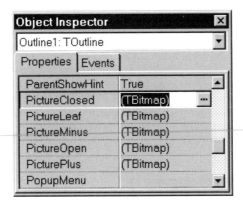

Fig. 15.19
*Changing **TOutline** properties*

These images are all defined by the five properties shown, which can each be different. Clicking on them invokes the picture editor.

 The **THeader** component (fig. 15.20) is used to display tabular information.

Fig. 15.20
*The **THeader** component*

The **Sections** property contains the headers. Type the headers into the Strings List Editor – one line per header. If the **AllowResize** property is true, the vertical line between the headers can be moved to re-size each section if the right mouse button is pressed. At run-time, the left mouse button must be used to re-size.

 The **TTabbedNotebook** component (fig. 15.21) is similar to using the **TTabSet** and the **TNoteBook** components together, except that it offers less flexibility, for example, in the positioning of the tabs. The **PageIndex** property allows you to select a particular page.

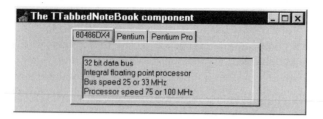

Fig. 15.21
*The **TabbedNoteBook**
component*

 The **TNoteBook** component (fig. 15.22) is used to display a set of pages, each of which may have its own controls. It is usually used in conjunction with the **TTabSet** component. Delphi makes extensive use of note books and tab set components. The currently active page is determined by the **ActivePage** property.

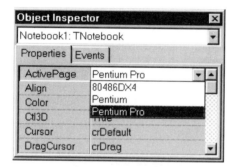

Fig. 15.22
*The properties of the **TNotebook** component*

The Data Access Page

Most of these components are covered in Chapter 14 on Database Access – but they are listed here to provide a complete reference.

 The **TDataSource** component connects the data aware controls to the underlying database.

 The **TTable** component provides access to a database using the Borland Database Engine (BDE).

 The **TQuery** component provides access to a database using SQL statements.

The **TStoredProc** component allows Delphi to execute stored applications. The **DataBaseName** property specifies the database in which the procedure is stored.

The **StoredProcName** property specifies the name of the stored procedure on the server.

 The **TDataBase** component is not required for database access, but provides some additional control for client–server applications. Delphi creates a **TDatabase** component that you cannot access when you open a database.

 The **TSession** component cannot be explicitly seen or created, but its properties and methods globally affect an application. A **TSession** component called Session is created everytime an application runs. The **DataBaseCount** and **Databases** properties specify the number and names of all active databases in the session.

 The **TBatchMove** component allows you to carry out actions on groups of records or on entire tables. The **Source** property specifies the dataset, either a **TQuery** or **TTable** component. The **Destination** property specifies a **TTable** component. The **Mode** property determines the operation to perform, append, update, copy and delete.

 The **TUpdateSQL** component encapsulates three **TQuery** components for updating a dataset.

The Data Controls Page

Most of the components on this page are duplicates of other components – the difference is that these components are data aware and can be used to contain information read from databases.

Many of these components have already been dealt with in Chapter 14 on Data Access but are listed here for completeness.

 The **TDBGrid** component accesses data in a database and displays it in a grid.

 The **TDBNavigator** component allows you to move around the database, selecting the next, previous, last or first record and deleting, updating and inserting records.

 The **TDBText** component has all the properties of a **TLabel** component.

 The **TDBEdit** component has all the properties of an **TEdit** component.

 The **TDBMemo** component has all the properties of a **TMemo** component.

The **TDBImage** component has all the properties of a **TImage** component.

 The **TDBListBox** component has all the properties of a **TListBox** component.

 The **TDBComboBox** component has all the properties of a **TComboBox** component.

 The **TDBCheckBox** component has all the properties of a **TCheckBox** component.

 The **TDBRadioButton** component has all the properties of a **TRadioButton** component.

 The **TDBLookupListBox** component has no equivalent non data aware component It is used to link two tables in a database that have a column in common; for example, a bank has a database with two tables, one with account details and the other with customer names and addresses. As you move down the table of account details, each customer is identified by a field containing the customer number. The second table contains the customer number and the address. This component allows you to link these two tables so that when you read the customer number in one table, the address can be looked up in the second table.

 The **TDBLookupComboBox** component has no equivalent data aware component. It behaves in the same way as the **TDBLookupList**, except that a combo box rather than a list box is displayed.

The Dialogs Page

The components on the Dialogs page make the Windows common dialog boxes available to your application. These Dialogs ensure that there is a family look to applications that carry out standard operations such as opening files.

 The **TOpenDialog** Component. This displays the familiar file opening dialog box. To display this dialog you must use the **Execute** method. For example, to display an open dialog box with the default name of OpenDialog1:

OpenDialog1.Execute;

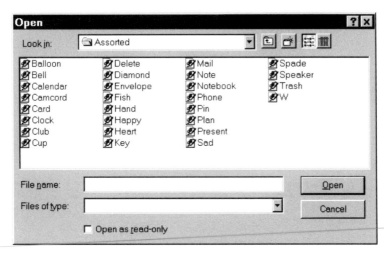

Fig. 15.23   *The **TOpenDialog** component*

The first unusual and unsatisfactory thing you notice about the dialog box in fig. 15.23 is that no files are listed in the File Name box or in the List Files of Type box. To get the files that you want to see displayed, you need to use the Filter editor (fig. 15.24). You can run this by clicking on the three dots adjacent to the **Filter** property.

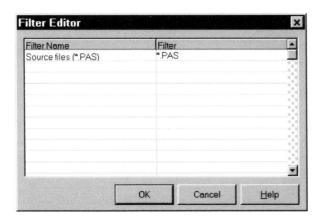

Fig. 15.24
The Filter editor

This option displays only files with a .PAS extension. The Filter name column is the text displayed in the List Files of Type box, while the entry in the Filter column appears in the File name box and ensures that only files of that type are displayed (fig. 15.25).

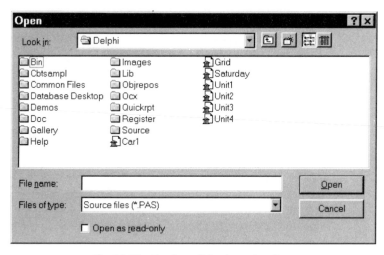

Fig. 15.25 *The Open dialog box using filters*

The File name box can be turned into a combo box by changing the **FileEditStyle** property to **fsComboBox** from **fsEdit**.

The name of the file selected is stored in the **FileName** property.

The **TSaveDialog** component (fig. 15.26) is very similar in appearance and behaviour to the **OpenDialog** box, except that it is used for saving files. It is invoked using the **Execute** method.

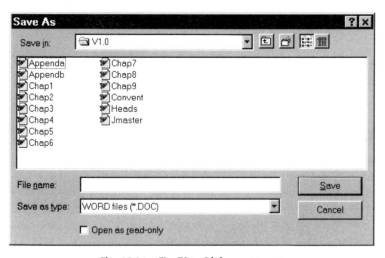

Fig. 15.26 *The **TSaveDialog** component*

A filter of DOC is specified and the **FileEditStyle** property is set to **fsComboBox**.

The **TOpenDialog** and the **TSaveDialog** dialog boxes have a large range of options which become visible if you click on the "+" symbol on the left of the **Options** property. The properties are by default set to false.

ofAllowMultiSelect: allows multiple files to be selected in the File name box.

ofCreatePrompt: you are prompted to create a new file if the one specified does not exist.

ofExtensionDifferent: if this is set to true by the application, the file selected has a different extension from the extension specified in the **DefaultExt** property.

ofFileMustExist: if a file name is entered that does not exist the application displays an error message and the user is prompted for the file name.

ofHideReadOnly: removes the ReadOnly check box from the dialog box.

OfNoChangeDir: prevents a change of directory or folder.

ofNoReadOnlyReturn: prevents the display or selection of read only files.

ofNoValidate: permits invalid file names to be specified.

ofOverWritePrompt: displays a dialog box before an existing file is overwritten.

OfReadOnly: checks the ReadOnly check box when the dialog is first displayed.

OfPathMustExist: an existing path name must be specified or an error dialog is displayed.

OfShareAware: ignores sharing errors.

OfShowHelp: shows a **Help** button on the dialog.

 The **TFontDialog** component (fig. 15.27) displays the available fonts. The **Font** property contains the selected font.

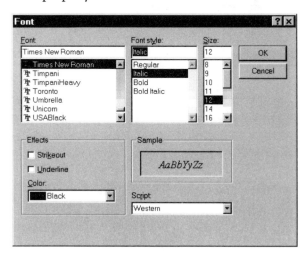

Fig. 15.27
*The **TFontDialog**
component*

This dialog also has a large number of sub properties which are displayed if you click on the **Options** property.

> **fdAnsiOnly**: only fonts that use the available Windows fonts can be selected.
> **fdEffects**: the Effects and Color portions of the dialog are not displayed.
> **fdFixedPitchOnly**: only mono-spaced fonts are displayed.
> **fdForceFontExist**: an error dialog box is displayed if an invalid font name is typed.
> **fdNoFaceSel**: an initial font name is not displayed.
> **fdNoVectorFonts**: only non-vector fonts are displayed.
> **fdNoSimulations**: GDI-simulation fonts are not displayed.
> **fdNoSizeSel**: an initial font size is not displayed.
> **fdNoStyleSel**: an initial style is not displayed.
> **fdNoOEMFonts**: same as **fNoVectorFonts**.
> **fdShowHelp**: displays a **Help** button.
> **fdtrueTypeOnly**: displays only true type fonts.
> **fdWysiwyg**: displays only fonts that are common to both screen and printer.

 The **TColorDialog** component (fig. 15.28).

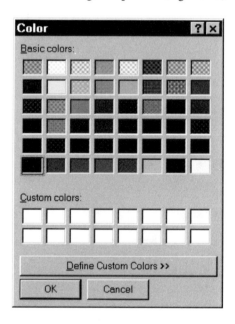

Fig. 15.28
The **TColorDialog** *component*

There are only three options for this component:

> **cdFullOpen**: the full display including custom colours, which you can define (as shown).

cdPreventFullOpen: does not display the Custom colours.
cdShowHelp: displays a **Help** button.

 The **TPrintDialog** component (fig. 15.29) permits you to specify the range of pages for printing. This uses the **FromPage** and **ToPage** properties.

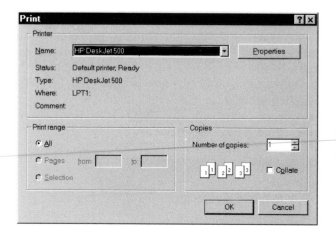

Fig. 15.29
The **TPrintDialog**
component

If you print to a file, the **PrintToFile** property is true.

 The **TPrinterSetupDialog** component (fig. 15.30) is used for specifying which printer to use and the attributes of that printer.

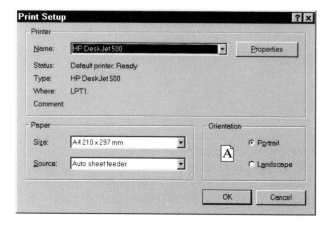

Fig. 15.30
The
TPrinterSetupDialog
component

This is a fully functioning dialog, including the **Options** button, the paper size and source, and the current printer. All this information is stored as part of your Windows 95 setup, which the dialog box accesses. The **TFindDialog** component (fig. 15.31) is a standard screen used in many applications, such as word processors or editors, which will initiate a search for the specified text.

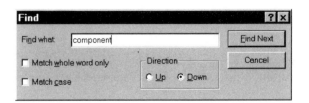

Fig. 15.31
*The **TFindDialog***
component

The text being searched for is in the **FindText** property. When the user chooses **FindNext**, the **OnFind** event occurs and it is in this event handler that you need to write code to take whatever action you want.

The **Options** property controls the type of search that is carried out, for example searching up or down the text.

The **TReplaceDialog** component (fig. 15.32) behaves in a very similar manner to the **TFindDialog** component.

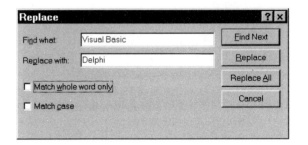

Fig. 15.32
*The **TReplaceDialog***
component

The text to be replaced is in the **ReplaceText** property. When the text is found, an **OnFind** event occurs.

The Systems Page

The **TTimer** component causes an **OnTimer** event when a specified period of time has occurred. The **Interval** property is used to specify the time. The component can be activated and deactivated using the **Enabled** property.

The **TPaintBox** component provides a rectangular area for you to paint on, rather than painting directly on the form. This component has its own **Canvas** that can be used as a drawing area.

The **TFileListBox** component (fig. 15.33) displays all the files in the current directory. To change the directory, change the value of the **Directory** property.

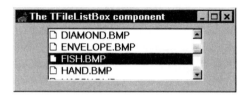

Fig. 15.33
The **TFileListBox** component

The **FileType** property controls the types of properties that are displayed based on their attributes. The nested properties are:

fdReadOnly: read-only files
ftHidden: hidden files
ftSystem: systems files
ftDirectory: directories
ftArchive: archived files
ftNormal: no attributes
ftVolumeID: displays the volume name.

These properties can be set to true or false. The files that are displayed can be further controlled by the **Mask** property. The default value is *.* which displays all files.

If you want to show a different icon alongside different file types, you can set the **ShowGlyphs** property to true. In the example shown, this property is set to true and the **FileType** property **ftDirectory** is set to true. The **TDirectoryListBox** component (fig. 15.34) displays the directory structure of the current disk drive. The **Drive** property controls which drive is current.

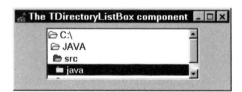

Fig. 15.34
The **TDirectoryListBox** component

When the **Drive** property changes, the **Directory** property changes to the current directory on that drive. It is useful to be able to synchronise changes in the component with changes in the **TFileListBox** component, so that when the directory changes the files displayed are those in the new directory. This needs just one line of code in the **OnChange** event for the directory list box:

```
procedure TForm1.DirectoryListBox1Change(Sender:TObject);
begin
    FileListBox1.Directory:= DirectoryListBox1.Directory
end;
```

The **TDriveComboBox** component (fig. 15.35) displays the list of available disk drives.

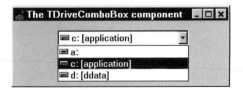

Fig. 15.35
The **TDriveComboBox** component

If you want to synchronise this component with a directory list box, you need a line of code in the **OnChange** event for this component:

> *procedure* *TForm1.DriveComboBox1Change(Sender:TObject);*
> *begin*
>   *DirectoryListBox1.**Directory**:= DriveComboBox1.**Drive***
> *end;*

 The **TFilterComboBox** component (fig. 15.36) displays all the available filters.

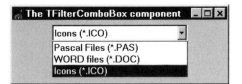

Fig. 15.36
The **TFilterComboBox**
component

The filters shown are described in the **Filter** property.

 The **TMediaPlayer** component (fig. 15.37) is used to control devices that provide a Media Control Interface (MCI). The component consists of a set of buttons that can control multi-media devices such as a VCR. It is beyond the scope of this book to go into more detail in this important but large area.

Fig. 15.37
The **TMediaPlayer**
component

 The **TOLEContainer** component (fig. 15.38) holds linked or embedded objects from another application. First create an OLE container and then click on its **ObjClass** property. This produces the screen shown, which prompts you for your OLE object.

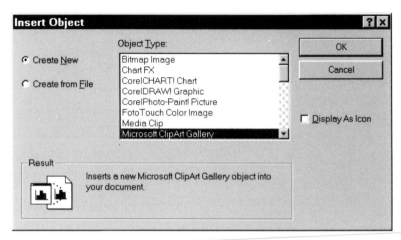

Fig. 15.38 The TOLEContainer component

In this example the **Create New** radio button is chosen, and the **Object Type** is Microsoft ClipArt Gallery. This runs the application and allows you to select your clipart image (fig. 15.39).

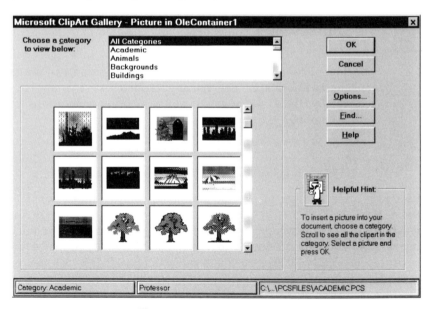

Fig. 15.39 Inserting an OLE object

When you choose it and click on OK, the **TOLEContainer** component (fig. 15.40) is seen to contain the selected image.

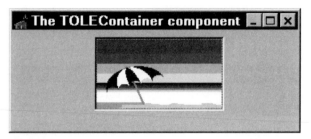

Fig. 15.40 *The TOLEContainer component with the ClipArt object*

There is a lot more to using OLE, but it is a large and complex area which is beyond the scope of this text.

 The **TDDEClientConv** component

 The **TDDEClientItem** component

 The **TDDEServerConv** component

 The **TDDEServerItem** component.

The four Dynamic Data Exchange (DDE) components are used for exchanging information between applications. DDE has now largely been replaced by OLE as the preferred way of allowing applications to interact with each other.

The OCX Page

VBX files could be used to provide additional controls in version 3 of Visual Basic. Many VBX files have been produced by third parties for increasing the functionality of the development environment and for providing a quick way of carrying out common operations that were not catered for in that development environment. Delphi 1.0 allowed you to use VBX files which meant that you could take advantage of the enormous range of components (controls in Visual Basic) that were available. In version 4 of Visual Basic, designed for Windows 95, VBX files were replaced with 32-bit versions called OCX files. In Delphi 2.0 VBX files have also been replaced with OCX files. As yet many companies have not provided 32-bit versions of existing VBX files, but are increasingly doing so. An OCX file is really a DLL (Dynamic Link Library) and is an ideal way of adding extra functionality to an existing application, such as the Delphi development environment without the need to create a new version.

The **TChartFX** component is the only OCX file supplied as a standard with all versions of Delphi 2. It is a powerful two- or three-dimensional charting tool (fig 15.41).

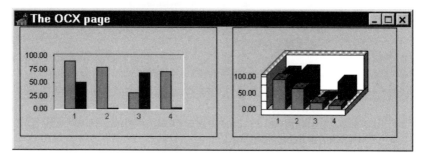

Fig. 15.41 *The OCX page*

The Samples Page

The **Samples** Page consists of a number of components that are built out of other standard components. The full source code for these components is distributed as a part of the standard Delphi implementation.

 The **TGauge** component (fig. 15.42) is a variant on the standard gauge component. The main difference is the **Kind** property which controls the type of gauge component:

    gkText: a rectangle containing a progress string
    gkHorizontalBar: a horizontal bar
    gkVerticalbar: a vertical bar
    gkPie: a pie chart with the progress expressed as a slice of pie
    gkNeedle: a clockwise rotating needle.

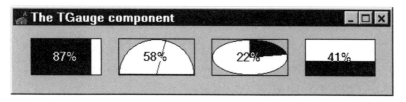

Fig. 15.42 *The **TGauge** component*

    The position of the gauge is controlled by the **Progress** property.
 The **TColorGrid** component (fig. 15.43) allows you to select a foreground colour by left clicking and a background by right clicking.

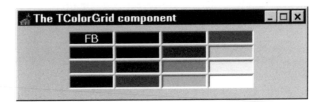

Fig. 15.43
The *TColorGrid*
component

The **GridOrdering** property controls the way in which the pattern of colours is displayed, for example, **go4x4** shows 4 rows and 4 columns.

The **TSpinButton** component (fig. 15.44) consist of nothing but a single up arrow and a single down arrow.

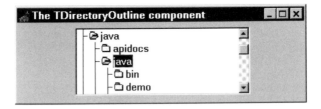

Fig. 15.44
The *TSpinButton* and
TSpinEdit component

The **TSpinEdit** component is similar to the **TSpinButton** component, except that it has an associated edit box.

The **TDirectoryOutline** component (fig. 15.45) displays the directories of the current disk in a hierarchical tree structure.

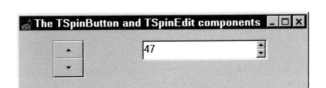

Fig. 15.45
The *TDirectoryOutline*
component

If you click on directory name and there are sub-directories, these are displayed.

The **TCalender** component (fig. 15.46) displays a calendar.

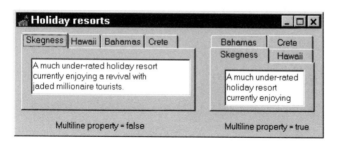

Fig. 15.46
The *TCalender*
component

By selecting the **Day, Month** and **Year** properties, you can control the month that is displayed.

The Win 95 Page

The **TTabControl** component is the Windows 95 version of the **TTabset** component which is used in Windows 3.1 and 3.11 applications. It behaves it the same way, providing a way of displaying multiple pages with a single dialog box as shown in fig 15.47.

Fig. 15.47
The *TTabControl*
component.

The **Tabs** property determines the caption of the pages, each line of the property creates a new page with a different heading. If a **TTabControl** is not enabled, all pages are disabled since this is a single control. If you want to have greater control over individual pages use the **TPageControl**. The **TabIndex** property determines which page is currently viewed and the **FirstIndex** property controls which tab is visible when the control is first displayed. A useful property is the **MultiLine** property which allows pages to be stacked.

The **TPageControl** component is the Windows 95 version of the **TTab-bedNoteBook** component used in Windows 3.1 and 3.11 applications. This component creates multiple overlapping pages each of which is a **TTabSet** component. To create new pages click on the right mouse button while over the **TPageControl** component and select the **New Page** option. Each of the pages can be accessed separately using the **PageIndex**

property. The key difference between the **TPageControl** and **TTabControl** is that individual pages can be enabled and disabled and have different properties in the **TPageControl** component since each of the pages is a different component. In the **TTabControl** each of the pages are a part of the same component.

 The **TTreeView** component is used to display hierarchical information. The text displayed is associated with the **Items** property. Clicking on this property in the Object Inspector displays the TreeView Items Editor as shown in fig 15.48.

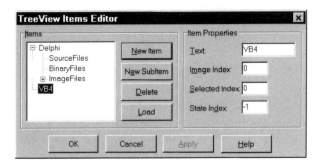

Fig. 15.48
The TTreeView Items Editor

Entries are entered using the **New Item** and **New SubItem** buttons. The text of the entry is stored in the **Text** property. When you have made a number of subindex entries and want to make an entry at a higher level, click on an entry at the level you want (this will collapse the branch below that entry) and select **New Item**. The **TTreeView** component in a running application is shown in fig 15.49.

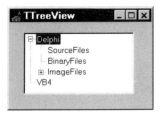

Fig. 15.49
Using the TTreeView component

To expand a branch click on the '+' sign, for example adjacent to the *ImageFiles* entry. To collapse an entry click on the '-' sign, for example adjacent to the *Delphi* entry. If you want to sort the sub-menu entries in alphabetical order set the **SortType** property to **stText**. Entries can be referenced using the **Items** property, for example *TreeView1.Items[2]* will reference the third entry. The first entry is *TreeView1.Items[0]*.

 The **TListView** component allows a list of items to be displayed in columns, with a header if required. Alternatively items may be displayed in rows or columns with or without associated icons. Clicking on the **Items** property allows you to enter, modify and delete items in the list.

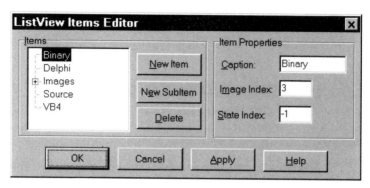

Fig. 15.50 *The ListView Items Editor*

If the **ViewStyle** property is set to **vsSmallIcon** or **vsIcon**, the **Image Index** property specified in the ListView Items Editor refers to the **ImageList** component assigned to the **SmallIcons** or **LargeIcons** property, and determines which image is displayed alongside each entry. If the **ViewStyle** property is set to **vsReport** and the **ShowColumnHeaders** property to true the list is displayed with headings.

 The **TImageList** component is a container for a group of images which are the same size. Each image can be referenced by its **Index** property. The default list size of 16x16, can be changed using the **Height** and **Width** properties. Images can be added using the **Add** method. In order to draw onto a specified canvas use the **DrawOverlay** method. One use for the **TImageList** component is that it is used to supply the images for the **TListView** component if icons are required alongside the text in the list displayed.

 The **THeaderControl** component is similar to the **THeader** component and provides a header bar. The text which goes into the headings is contained in the **Sections** property. Clicking on this property displays the HeaderControl Sections Editor as shown in fig 15.51.

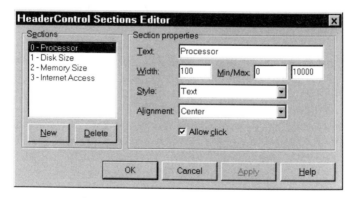

Fig. 15.51 *The HeaderControl Sections Editor*

If the *Allow click* box is checked for a section the **OnSectionClick** event is enabled. The position of the component is determined by the **Align** property, and the header may be displayed along any edge of the form. Fig 15.52 shows the component aligned along the top of the form.

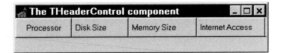

| Processor | Disk Size | Memory Size | Internet Access |

Fig. 15.52
Using the
THeaderControl
component

The **TRichEdit** component is an extremely useful component which meets a real demand among users. It is a variation on the **TMemo** component and allows a rich text format to be used. You can change the formatting of individual characters or words, for example, changing the character size or font, the tab positions, or the alignment. Automatic drag drop of text is also supported.

The example below shows a rich text box containing text in different styles.

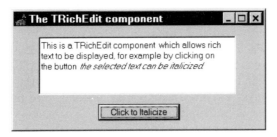

Fig. 15.53
The **TRichEdit** *component*

The only code needed is in the button click event is shown below:

```
procedure TForm1.Button1Click(Sender: TObject);
begin
    if richedit1.SelAttributes.Style <> [fsitalic] then
    richedit1.SelAttributes.Style := [fsitalic] else
    richedit1.SelAttributes.Style := [];
end;
```

The **TStatusBar** component is a window which may be either horizontal or vertical along any edge of a window and is used for displaying status information. The position is determined by the **Align** property. This component is divided into a collection of panels within the **Panel** property. Each panel has its own set of formatting properties and text. The number of panels is given by the **Count** property.

The **TTrackBar** component (fig 15.54) can be either horizontal or vertical (the **Orientation** property). Optional tick marks can be added by setting the **TickMarks** property The **Position** property gives the number of ticks between the **Min** and **Max** properties.

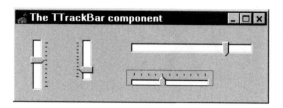

Fig. 15.53
The **TTrackBar** component

The **LineSize** property determines how many ticks are moved by the arrowed keys, while the **PageSize** property gives the number of ticks moved by pressing PageUp or PageDown keys or clicking on the bar.

 The **TProgressBar** component is used to give an indication to the user of how far a process has progressed. It has similar properties to the **TTrackBar** component, in particular the **Position** property gives the progression of the process between the **Min** and **Max** values. The **Step** property determines how much to change the **Position** property by every time it changes when the **StepIt** method is invoked for the progress bar.

The **TUpDown** component is simply a pair of arrowed keys, one pointing up, the other down. Every time the up arrow is pressed the **Position** property is increased by one. **Position** is decremented every time the down arrow is pressed. This component is usually connected to another control called a buddy window. The **Associate** property specifies the buddy window.

The **THotKey** component is used to assign a shortcut key at run time. The user enters the key combination, for example **Ctrl+a**. This hot key is connected to a property of another control by assigning the **HotKey** property to the property of the associated control that you want to invoke.

16

Pascal Primer

Introduction

The background language for Delphi is Object Pascal. If you have programmed in Pascal before, you can skim through most of this chapter, but there are likely to be several features that you may not know about.

The special features of Object Pascal related to the object orientation aspects of the language and how it differs from "standard" Pascal is covered in Chapter 17.

In this chapter you will learn about:

- The structure of Pascal programs.
- Declaring identifiers.
- Assignment statements.
- Controlling program flow.
- Defining your own data types.
- Using arrays and records.

Program Structure

Programs in Object Pascal are made up of collections of statements grouped together into procedures or functions.

Program Layout

Programs can be confusing to read if they all start at the same column number, especially if there are loops. It is a good idea to use the convention of stepping in a tab position every time a new block of code starts, for example:

```
var
    count: integer;
begin
    Canvas.Pen.Style := psdashdot;
    Canvas.Pen.Color = RGB(120,120,200);
    for count := 1 to 5 do
    begin
        Canvas.Pen.Width := count;
        Canvas.MoveTo(20, count*20);
        Canvas.LineTo(200, count*20);
    end;
end;
```

This section of a program draws five lines of varying width on the default form. **Begin**s and **end**s are on their own lines and **begin...end** pairs are at the same tab position. It is good to develop your own style, but the method shown is widely used and makes your code easier to read.

Data Types

Object Pascal offers a wide range of standard data types and also allows you to define your own.

Data Type	Number of Bytes	Description
Integer	2	Integer from − 32,768 to 32,767
Shortint	1	Integer from − 128 to 127
Longint	4	Integer from − 2,147,483,647 to 2,147,483,647
Byte	1	Integer from 0 to 255
Word	2	Integer from 0 to 65 535
Single	4	Floating Point. 7 or 8 significant digits in the fractional part.
Double	8	Floating Point. 15 or 16 significant digits.
Extended	10	Floating Point. 19 or 20 significant digits.
Real	6	Floating Point. 11 or 12 significant digits.
Currency	19–20	Fixed point for monetary calculations.
Boolean	1	true or false.
Char	1	An ASCII character.
String	0 to 255	A list of characters.
Pointer	2	A pointer to an unspecified type.
PChar	2	A pointer to a null-terminated string.
Variant	–	Becomes the data type it is assigned.

The **Real** type is only included for compatibility with earlier releases of Borland Pascal and should be avoided if possible.

Operators

Object Pascal has a full complement of operators for:

- Arithmetic
- Comparison
- Logical operations
- Bitwise operations.

There are six arithmetic operators:

Operator	Description
+	Add.
−	Subtract.
*	Multiply.
/	Divide.
div	Integer division.
mod	The remainder after dividing two integers.

The standard set of relational and assignment operator is provided:

Operator	Description
:=	Assignment.
=	Test for equality.
>	Greater than.
>=	Greater than or equal to.
<	Less than.
<=	Less than or equal to.
<>	Not equal.

If you want to test for equality between two identifiers, use = ; if you want to do an assignment, use := . For example:

```
if c = 99 then exit( );     {tests to see if c is equal to 99 and exits if it is}
c := 99;                    {assigns c the value 99}
```

These operators can be used on strings as well as numerical values. Object Pascal also has the usual set of logical or boolean operators:

Operator	Description
not	Negation.
and	Logical and.
or	Logical or.
xor	Logical exclusive or.

Unlike the other logical operators, **not** is applied to only one boolean identifier, for example:

```
var
    found : boolean
begin
    found := file_search(filename);
    If (not found) then ShowMessage('File not found');
end;
```

The boolean *found* is returned by the procedure *file_search*, which searches for a file. If the value of *found* is false, the value of *not found* is true and the message box is displayed.

The **and** operator checks to see if both of the supplied values are true; if they are, then a value of true is generated.

```
if (memory_size <= 4) and (processor speed < 25) then
begin
    ShowMessage('Not ideal for Windows 95');
end;
```

In this code fragment, if the memory size is less than or equal to 4 Mb **and** the processor speed is less than 25 MHz, then this is not an ideal machine for Windows 95.

The inclusive or (**or**) and the exclusive or (**xor**) are very similar. They both return a false value if both of the supplied values are false. They both return a value of true if either of the values is true. The difference is that if both values are true, **or** will return a value of true while **xor** will return a value of false. For example:

```
if (age < 25) or (engine_size >2000) then
begin
    ShowMessage('there will be an extra car insurance premium');
end;
```

It is correct to use **or** in this example; if the age of the car driver is under 25 or the engine size is over 2000 cc, or if both of these conditions are true, then there is an extra insurance premium. If you used **xor** in this case, drivers who are both under 25 and have cars with large engines would not be charged a higher premium.

Bitwise operators

Object Pascal has six bitwise operators which operate directly on the bit patterns of the variables:

Operator	Description
not	Bitwise negation.
and	Bitwise and.
or	Bitwise inclusive or.
xor	Bitwise exclusive or
shl	Bitwise shift left.
shr	Bitwise shift right.

The **not** operator changes all the bits with a value of 1 to 0 and those with a value of 0 to 1. For example:

```
var
    first, second : integer;
begin
    first := 57;              { the bit pattern for 57 is 0000 0000 0011 0001 }
    second := not value1; { the bit pattern for second is 1111 1111 1100 1110}
end;
```

A useful way of showing what effect these logical operators have on the bits is to make a truth table that gives all the four possible combinations of bits:

bit 1	bit 2	bit 1 and bit 2
0	0	0
0	1	0
1	0	0
1	1	1

Similarly for the **or** and **xor** operators:

bit 1	bit 2	bit 1 or bit 2	bit 1 xor bit 2
0	0	0	0
0	1	1	1
1	0	1	1
1	1	1	0

The shift left and shift right operators have a different operation. A shift left by one place has the effect of multiplying the value by 2. A shift of two places multiplies by 4, a shift of three places by 8, and so on.

The shift right operator behaves in a similar way, except that it is effectively a division by 2 for every place shifted.

```
value :=26;
result := value shr 1;
```

gives a value of 13 for result. If this is shifted left again, it gives a value of 6.

```
value := 17;
result := value shl 3;
```

gives a value of 68;

Declaring Variables

Identifiers are the names of variables, functions, procedures, methods, and so on which are used in an application. In Object Pascal, before an identifier is used, it must be declared. When you declare an identifier, you must declare its name and also its type.

Variable declarations are preceded with the reserved word **var**. For example:

```
var
    name: string;
    address : string;
    age : integer;
```

If you have more than one variable of a type to declare, you can put them on the same line:

```
var
    name, address : string;
    age : integer;
```

Put the variable declaration of variable after the start of the procedure and before the start of the executable program.

```
procedure TForm1.Button1Click(Sender: TObject);
var
    value1, value2, total : single;
begin
    value1 := 3;
    value2 := 5;
    total := value1 + value2;
end
```

This procedure is the button click event for *Button1*. The two input values are added together.

Declaring Constants

To declare a constant, the keyword **const** is used. For example:

```
const
     Array_size = 512;
     My_text = 'Object Pascal';
     Value = 3*60*60;
```

This is followed by the name of the constant and its value. You can have mathematical expressions that can be calculated at compile time.

```
Var
     count;
Const
     result = 7 * count;
```

However, this is not a legal declaration since it cannot be calculated until run-time.

Converting Between Types

The next program has some new features: it calculates the area of a circle when you type the radius and click on the calculate button. The running program is shown in fig. 16.1.

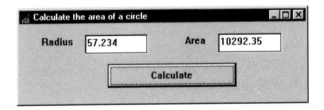

Fig. 16.1
Type conversions

You need to declare a constant, *pi*; that is, a value that cannot be changed while the program is running. This is done in the **const** section at the top of the procedure. You do not need to declare the type of the constant, since Object Pascal can work out what type is required from the value assigned to the constant.

The radius is typed into an edit box and is stored in the **Text** property of that edit box. The problem is that **Text** property stores a string that needs to be converted to an floating point value before it can be operated on. The **StrToFloat** function does this conversion. When the area has been calculated, it must be converted into a string to be displayed in the second edit box. There is a companion function called **FloatToStr** that does the conversion. The whole of the event handler for the button **OnClick** event looks like this:

```
procedure TForm1.Button1Click(Sender: TObject);
const
     pi = 3.142;
```

```
var
      radius, area : real;
begin
      radius := StrToFloat(edit1.Text);
      area := pi * radius * radius;
      edit2.Text := FloatToStr(area);
end;
```

There are a number of other functions used for converting between different types of data and they all behave in the same way.

Function name	Description
IntToStr	Integer to string.
StrToInt	String to integer.
IntToHex	Integer to string in hexadecimal format.
HexToStr	Hexadecimal number to string.
StrToDate	String to date.
DateToStr	Date to string.
StrToTime	String to time.
TimeToStr	Time to string.

The time and date functions return the current time and date. If you want to display either of these, for instance, in a label box, you must convert them to a string. For example:

```
label1.Caption := DateToStr(Date);
label2.Caption := TimeToStr(Time);
```

Calling Procedures and Functions

If you want to use a procedure, you need to call it. You do this by putting the name of the procedure in your program. For instance, if you want to take different action depending on the age of a person, you can do this by having a different action specified in a set of procedures. For example:

```
if (income >40000) then
begin
      if (age < 35 ) then yuppy_mailshot( )
      else if (age > 75) then crumbly_mailshot( )
      else if (age > 60) then wrinkly_mailshot( )
      else if (age > 35) then ex_yuppy_mailshot( );
end;
```

```
procedure yuppy_mailshot ( )
{ send these customers details of timeshares }
var
........
```

This is an excerpt from a program used by a marketing company which sends out different information to high income people depending on their age.

If you want to call a method associated with a control, you need to specify the name of the control and the method. For example;

button1.OnClick

calls the **OnClick** event handler for the button called *button1*. This is really just a call to a procedure.

Passing Parameters

Sometimes you need to pass information between a calling procedure and a called procedure. You do this by passing parameters. For example, these two procedures help you to choose what to do on a Saturday night:

```
procedure get_a_life
var
    what_to_do : integer;
begin
    what_to_do := Random(5));
    show_choice(what_to_do);
end;
```

This procedure generates a random number between 0 and 4; it then passes the value to the procedure *show_choice* as an integer.

```
procedure show_choice(what_to_do : integer);
begin
    case what_to_do of
    0: ShowMessage('Party');
    1: ShowMessage('Clean the kitchen floor');
    2: ShowMessage('Go for a meal');
    3: ShowMessage('Rave');
    4: ShowMessage('Watch Star Trek video');
    end;
end;
```

When the program is run, it displays one of a number of possible messages (fig. 16.2).

Fig. 16.2
"What to do on Saturday night"

The *show_choice* procedure receives one parameter which it does not change, but sometimes you do want to change a value in the called procedure and pass it back. For example, if you want to calculate the average of three numbers and pass the result back:

```
var
     average, value1, value2, value3 : single;
begin
     get_average (average, value1, value2, value3);
     edit1.Text := IntToStr(average);;
end;
```

```
procedure get_average(var av: single, val1, val2, val3 : single)
begin
     av := (val1 + val2 + val3)/3;
end;
```

In this code the three identifiers *val1*, *val2* and *val3* remain unchanged, while the identifier *av* is changed in the called procedure and the result passed back.

val1, *val2* and *val3* are passed by value; that is, a copy of the current value of the identifier is passed to the called routine. The first parameter is passed by address, and can be changed in the called procedure. It is preceded by the keyword **var** in the called procedure.

Note that the names of the parameters in the calling and called procedures does not have to be the same. The first parameter in the calling list refers to the first parameter in the called routine, and so on.

Using Functions

It is rather clumsy passing a variable to a procedure so that it can be changed and passed back, and sometimes it is better to call a function rather than a procedure.

```
var
     average, value1, value2, value3 : single;
begin
     average := get_average( value1, value2, value3);
     edit1.Text := IntToStr(average);
end;
```

```
function get_average( val1, val2, val3 : integer) : single
begin
    get_average := (val1 + val2 + val3)/3;
end;
```

Note that the function **IntToStr** is used here to convert from an integer to a string.

```
var
    val1, val2, val3, total : integer;
begin
    total := val1 + val2 + val3;
    my_text := IntToStr(total);
end;
```

This code adds three integers together and calls **IntToStr** to convert the integer to a string which it assigns to the **Text** property of a text box called *my_text*.

Controlling Program Flow

There are two branching statements in Object Pascal:

- **If Then Else** Statement.
- **Case** statement.

and three looping statements

- **Repeat.**
- **While.**
- **For.**

If Then Else Statements

The simplest form of an **if then** statement is:

```
if (age<18) then ShowMessage('you cannot vote yet');
```

This can be complemented by an **else** statement:

```
if (Bankbalance < 0) then
    ShowMessage ('Overdrawn')
else
    ShowMessage ('In credit');
```

You can have nested **if** statements to make multiple levels of decision. For example:

```
if (memory < 8) then
    begin
    if (processor_speed < 66)) then
        begin
            if (disk_size < 100) then ShowMessage('Don't run
                Windows 95');
        end;
    end;
```

This is a confusing piece of code. It is much better to write:

```
if (memory <8) and (processor_speed < 66) and (disk_size <100) then
    ShowMessage('Don't run Windows 95');
```

You can use nested **else** clauses, but this can make even more confusing code than nested **if** statements when carried to extremes.

```
procedure processor_choice( processor : Integer);
begin
    if processor = Pentium then
        edit1.Text := 'Ideal Windows platform'
    else
        if processor = Intel486 then
            edit1.Text := 'Fine for Windows'
        else
            if processor = Intel386 then
                edit1.Text := 'Recommend upgrade for Windows';
end;
```

This example puts some different text into the text box depending on the type of processor you are using.

Note that no semicolons are used until the end of the last **else** clause.

Case Statements

The **case** statement is a useful alternative to using multiple **else** statements. For example:

```
procedure size_of_memory(memory : integer);
begin
    case memory of
        2 : edit1.Text := 'Not enough memory';
        4,6 : edit1.Text := 'Barely enough memory';
        8 : edit1.Text := 'Enough memory';
        12,16,20,24,28,32 : edit1.Text := 'Ample memory';
    else
```

```
        edit1.Text := 'More than enough memory'; { >32 Mb of memory}
    end;
end;
```

If the size of the memory, as passed in the parameter memory, is 2 Mb there is *Not enough memory*; 4 or 6 Mb is *barely enough*; 8 is *enough*; and 12, 16, 20, 24, 28 and 32 are *Ample*. If none of these conditions apply, then the identifier is greater than 32 Mb (since the smallest memory chips are now 4 Mb). The text is assigned to the **Text** property of *Edit1*.

The only drawback is that the identifier used (in this case *memory*) can only be either an integer (but not **Longint**), a char, or an enumerated type. Enumerated types are covered later.

Repeat Statements

The **Repeat** statement allows a set of instructions to be repeated until a condition is met. This code displays a countdown timer in an edit box. It uses the **TTimer** component (fig. 16.3).

Fig. 16.3.   *The **TTimer** component is the leftmost component on the Systems page of the components palette.*

When the timer expires, an **OnTimer** event occurs; this is used to update the countdown in the edit box. The **Interval** property of the timer is used to assign the countdown time in milliseconds to start the timer. Setting the **Interval** property at the end of the **OnTimer** event, if the count is not zero, initiates another **OnTimer** event in one second.

```
procedure TForm1.Timer1Timer(Sender: TObject);
begin
    Count := 10;
    repeat
        edit1.Text := IntToStr(count);
        count := count - 1;
        timer1.Interval := 1000;
    until (count >= 0);
end;
```

This code displays a timer which counts down from 10 to 0.

The statements within a **Repeat** block are always executed at least once, since the terminating condition is not checked until the end of the block.

While Statements

While statements are similar to **Repeat** statements except that the terminating condition is checked at the start – so the statements within the **while** block may not execute even when the termination condition is met.

```
count := 10;
while count >= 0 do
begin
    timer1. Interval := 1000;
    edit1.Text := IntToStr(count);
    count := count - 1;
end;
```

This does exactly the same as the **Repeat** loop. Note that the code within the **While** clause is enclosed by a **begin end** pair.

For Statements

It is common to want to change the value of an identifier every time a loop is executed. The **for** statement does this. For example:

```
for count :=10 downto 0 do
begin
    timer. Interval := 1000;
    edit1.Text := IntToStr(count);
end;
```

This does exactly the same as the previous two examples. The **for** statements initialises *count* to 10 and decreases it every time the loop is executed. If you want the loop counter to increase from 0 to 10, you substitute the reserved word **downto** for **do**:

```
for count := 0 to 10 do
```

You need to enclose the code within the loop by a **begin...end** pair if there is more than one statement. If there is only one statement, you do not need to do this:

```
for count :=1 to 20 do
    edit1.Text := IntToStr(Count);
edit2.Text := 'The loop has ended';
```

Defining Data Types

In addition to the standard data types, Object Pascal allows you to define your own data types. The main categories of user defined data types are:

- Enumerated types
- Subrange types
- Arrays
- Records.

Enumerated Types

An enumerated type lists all the possible values that a variable of that type can have. For example:

type
>*Tweek_days = (Monday, Tuesday, Wednesday, Thursday, Friday);*
>*Tweekend = (Saturday, Sunday);*

These statements define two data types of type *Tweek_days* and *Tweekend*. They both start with a capital *T* to indicate that they are types; this is not compulsory but it is a useful convention to use. Before you can use these types, you need to create some identifiers of these types, in the same way as you need to create identifiers of standard types such as **integer** and **single** before using them.

var
>*day : Tweek_days;*

You can then make assignments or tests using the declared variable:

today := Tuesday;
if (day = Monday) **then** *start_of_week( );*

Underlying these enumerated types are an integer data structure, but it is easier to use enumerated types to give meaningful names such as the days of the week rather than using the alternative:

var
>*day : integer;*
begin
>*day := 2;*
>*if (day = 1)* **then** *start_of_week ( );*

Enumerated types can be very useful, particularly when you are using radio buttons to specify your choice (fig. 16.4).

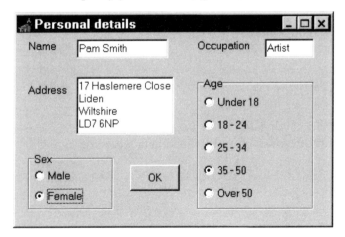

Fig. 16.4
Using enumerated types

In this application, the user has to specify sex and also age; the user can only choose one of each. The enumerated types look like this:

```
type
    Tgender = (Male, Female);
    Tage = (aunder18, a18to25, a26-35, a36to50, aover50);
var
    age : Tage;
    gender : Tgender;
```

The types follow the convention of starting with the letter *T*.

In the event handler for the **TRadioGroup** component, you can find out what selection has been made. For example:

```
if (radiogroup1.itemIndex = 1) then gender := Female;
if (radiogroup1.itemIndex = 0) then gender := Male;
```

There is only one **OnClick** event handler for all the radio buttons in a group; you distinguish which button has been clicked by looking at the **ItemIndex** property, which is zero for the first radio button, one for the second, and so on.

Subrange Types

Subrange types allow you to limit the range of an existing integer, char, boolean or enumerated type. For example, if your application is asking how many hours you worked yesterday, it expects a number between 1 and 24 hours (it just feels like more sometimes!).

```
Type
    Thours_worked = 0..24;
    Tlower_case = 'a'..'z';
    Tprocessors = (8086, 80286, 80386, 80486, Pentium);
    Tprocessors_for_windows = 80386..Pentium;
```

Thours is an integer type with a value between 0 and 24, and *Tlower_case* is a character between "a" and "z". *Tprocessors* is a definition of an enumerated type of a list of processors. *Tprocessors_for_windows* is a list of the processors from the 80386 through to Pentium.

The next application creates a type of integers between 0 and 24:

```
type
    thours = 0..24;
var
    hours : thours;
```

The running program is shown in fig. 16.5.

Fig. 16.5   *Range checking*

When you click the button, the text in the edit box is converted to an integer.

hours := StrToInt(edit1.Text);

An error message is displayed if the value is outside the specified range. If the error message does not appear, you have not enabled the run-time checking. This is a an option that is under the **Options** option of the **Project** menu. Choose the Compiler page and click on **Range checking** under **Runtime errors.**

Arrays

An array is a set of data items of the same type. If you want to save a list of values, an array is an ideal choice. For example, to save a list of costs:

var
    *costs : **array[1..5] of** single;*

This defines a one-dimensional array with five elements, the first element is referred to as *costs*[1], and the last as *costs*[5]. These array elements are used in the same way as other identifiers. The benefit of having them in an array is that they can be referred to very easily using looping constructs:

sum :=, 0;
*for count =1 **to** 5 **do***
    sum := sum + cost[count];

A special type of one-dimensional array is used for storing strings. For example:

*name_string : **string[10];***

This creates a string of 10 characters.
Arrays can have many dimensions, but the most useful ones have either one or two dimension. For example:

var
> *table : **array** [1..5,1..5] of integer;*

This can be especially useful when accessing a grid. The **Cells** property of a grid contains the contents of the cells. Rows and columns are both numbered from 0 upwards, with the top left corner as the 0,0 position. The grid shown has been used to display an exercise program (fig. 16.6).

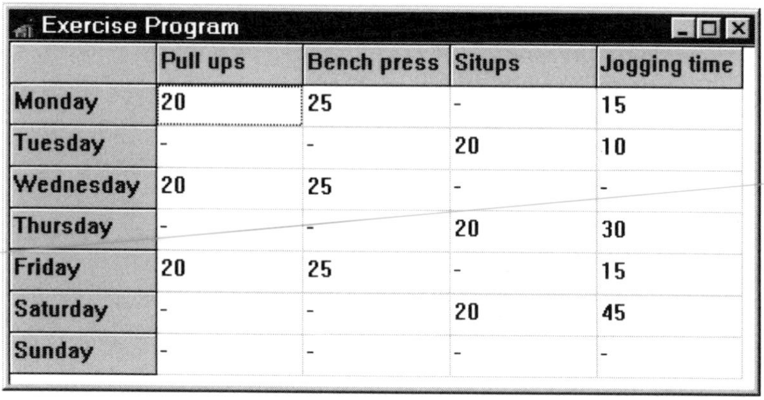

Exercise Program	Pull ups	Bench press	Situps	Jogging time
Monday	20	25	-	15
Tuesday	-	-	20	10
Wednesday	20	25	-	-
Thursday	-	-	20	30
Friday	20	25	-	15
Saturday	-	-	20	45
Sunday	-	-	-	-

Fig. 16.6 *Using grids*

The individual cells can be loaded at run-time as follows:

```
StringGrid1.Cells[0,1] := 'Monday';
StringGrid1.Cells[0,2] := 'Tuesday';
StringGrid1.Cells[0,3] := 'Wednesday';
StringGrid1.Cells[0,4] := 'Thursday';
StringGrid1.Cells[0,5] := 'Friday';
StringGrid1.Cells[0,6] := 'Saturday';
StringGrid1.Cells[0,7] := 'Sunday';
```

and so on for all the cells in the grid.

If you want to find out the maximum amount of jogging that you did in a week, you can use the code:

```
var
    most : integer;
begin
    most := 0;
    for (c=0 to (StringGrid1.RowCount - 1)) do
    if StringGrid1.Cells[4,c] < most then most := StringGrid1.Cells[4,c];
```

The **RowCount** property of the grid gives the number of rows (the **ColCount** property gives the number of columns). The identifier *most* contains the greatest number of minutes you have jogged for.

Records

A record is a collection of items of data which may be of different types. For example, you may wish to create a record that contains details of a computer:

```
type
    TComputer = record
        processor : string[7];
        clock_speed : integer;
        memory : integer;
        cost : single;
    end;
```

You can now create data items of type *TComputer*:

```
var
    my_computer, your_computer : TComputer;
```

You can refer to individual elements of the identifier my_computer. For example:

```
my_computer.processor := '486';
my_computer.clock_speed := 100;
my_computer.memory := 16;
my_computer.cost := 1200;
```

Specify the name of the identifier, followed by the name of the component you want to refer to. A useful short-hand way of assigning values is to use the **with** statement:

```
with your_computer do
    begin
        processor := 'Pentium';
        clock_speed := 133;
        memory := 32;
        cost := 2300;
    end;
```

Delphi has a very flexible programming language, with a wide range of data types and strong data type check which is invaluable in reducing bugs. In addition to this, it also has a strong object oriented aspect. Some Delphi programmers choose to ignore the object orientation of Delphi and use it as a visual Pascal, but it is worth spending time finding out about object orientation, since it does help you to write bug free Windows applications faster, which is what Delphi is all about.

17

Object Pascal

Introduction

One of the key ways in which Delphi scores over languages such as Visual Basic is that it is object oriented. The Pascal engine in Delphi is based on the very successful Object Pascal from Borland.

What are Objects?

An object is a user defined type, like the record structures that we have looked at. The difference is that an object also has a set of operations or methods that can be carried out on those types.

You have already used objects throughout this book every time you created or used a component. Every component is an object, and the set of operations that you can perform on each component are the methods for that object. This is why the window that gives details of the properties of components is called the Object Inspector.

When you create an object, it can be used by other applications to increase productivity and to reduce errors.

The TForm Object

All objects have a type. For example, when you create a form, the default name for the first form is *form1* if it is of type **TForm1**, which is based on the type **TForm**. The template code for a form in file Unit1.Pas looks like this:

```
unit unit1;

interface

uses
     SysUtils, WinTypes, WinProcs, Messages, Classes, Graphics, Controls,

type
     TForm1 = class(TForm)
     private
          { Private declarations }
     public
          { Public declarations }
     end;

var
     form1: TForm1;

implementation

{$R *.DFM}

end.
```

This file is called a unit.

The form type is declared in the **var** section; all other sections are blank until another component is added.

If, for example, a button is added to the screen, this file becomes:

```
unit unit1;

interface

uses
     SysUtils, WinTypes, WinProcs, Messages, Classes, Graphics, Controls,
     Frms, Dialogs, StdCtrls;

type
     TForm1 = class(TForm)
          Button1: TButton;
          procedure Button1Click(Sender: TObject);
     private
          { Private declarations }
     public
          { Public declarations }
     end;
```

```
var
      form1: TForm1;

implementation

{$R *.DFM}

procedure TForm1.Button1Click(Sender: TObject);
begin
      ShowMessage('single click');
end;

end.
```

The main changes are that the **TForm1** object has a field called *Button1* of type **TButton.** All objects can contain other objects, and every time that a new component is added to the form, a new field is added to the **TForm1** type.

This file also contains the event code for the **OnClick** event for the button. This is a method for the form object.

In summary, the form called *Form1* is an object of type **TForm1**, derived from the **TForm** class and contains the **TButton1** object of type **TButton**. It has one method associated with it.

Object Classes

The new form called *Form1* is of type **TForm1**. This "inherits" all the properties of the **TForm** type. TForm is a standard type which is at the heart of all Delphi applications. The **TForm** object has a lot of properties that allows all forms of this type or of a type that inherits these properties to do a lot of things. For example, you can move forms around the screen, re-size and minimise them. You can see the properties and events associated with this type by using the on-line Help to search for **TForm**.

The declaration declaring this is present in Unit1.pas:

TForm1 = class(TForm)

Every time you create a new form, it has a type that is derived from the **TForm** type and has all the properties of this type which are used as a base for further properties to be added or removed. Every time you add a component (itself an object) to a form, you are changing the methods associated with that form and making it slightly different from **TForm** itself (fig. 17.1).

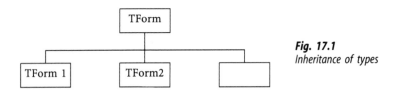

Fig. 17.1
Inheritance of types

TForm1 and any other based on **TForm** (all forms in Delphi!) are descendants of **TForm**.

TForm is called the ancestor of **TForm1**.

An object of a defined type is sometimes called an *instance*. For example, *Form1* is an instance of type *TForm1*.

Private and Public

If you want to refer, for example, to the property of a button from an event procedure of another component on the same form, you do not need to state explicitly which form the button is on. It is assumed that it is on the same form:

> **procedure** *TForm1.**Button1Click**(Sender: TObject);*
> **begin**
> > *ListBox1.**Clear**;*
> **End;**

clears the list box called *ListBox1* on *Form1*. The statement has the same effect as:

> *Form1.ListBox1.**Clear**;*

If you want to clear a list box on a form called *MyForm*, the correct statement is:

> *MyForm.ListBox1.**Clear**;*

Directly below the type declaration are the **Private** and **Public** directives.

The **Public** directive is used to declare data and methods that you want methods in other units to access.

By contrast, data and methods declared in the **Private** section are available only to the current unit. For example:

> **Private**
> > *mylist : **integer**;*
> > *name : **string**;*
>
> **Public**
> > *function get_colour(**int** xpos) : **integer**;*
> **end;**

The two identifiers declared are only available to objects within the current unit, while the function *get_colour* is accessible from any unit, however it must be referred to by its full name of *Form1.get_colour* if it is called from outside the current form.

Using the Is Operator

Object Pascal has strong type checking and, as you would expect, this applies to object variables. You can only assign an object variable to another of the same type, for example, if two forms are both derived from the same **TForm** class, you can assign them to each other:

    Form1 := Form2;

The above is a legal assignment statement. If you need to check the type of an object variable, you can use the **Is** operator. This returns a boolean variable which is true if the object is of the specified type. For example:

if (ActiveControl Is TButton) then ListBox1.Clear

The generalised form is:

If (objectref is classref) then .....

Object Orientation

There is a current trend in software development towards using object orientation. Delphi has the key elements that allow you to design your software in an object oriented way. The main benefits of this approach are that objects can be developed that contain both data and a set of operations that can be performed on that data. Since an object presents a fully defined interface to other objects, it is possible to build up a library of object modules. This makes it easier to reuse software. Provided that objects are thoroughly tested and debugged, this is a quicker way to develop complex applications than to start from the beginning with every application.

Delphi supports the current trends in software development not only of object orientation but also of event driven software in a Windows environment. It is these features combined with an excellent user interface that makes Delphi such a good development environment to use.

18
Delphi and Visual Basic

Introduction

If you had wanted to develop Windows applications a few years ago, before Delphi was available, Visual Basic was probably your best option. If you have used Visual Basic you have a head start in learning Delphi, but there are some major differences and some traps that you may fall into if you assume that things behave in the same way in both of these systems.

In this chapter you will learn about:

- Compiled versus interpreted code.
- Differences in string manipulation.
- Differences in type checking.
- Using databases.

The Development Environment

Since both Visual Basic and Delphi are designed for developing Windows programs, it is not surprising that they are so similar. Since all the available components (or controls as they are called in Visual Basic) are standard features of Windows, they are all available in slightly different forms on the two systems.

Delphi has a Component Palette while Visual Basic has a toolbox.

Delphi has an Object Inspector while Visual Basic has a Property window.

The events have similar names, for example, the **Click** event in Visual Basic is called the **OnClick** event in Delphi. The same range of events is available.

Delphi has a much wider range of components than Visual Basic, but virtually anything that you can do in Delphi you can do in Visual Basic, and vice versa.

The user interface in Delphi seems to be better, perhaps because it was developed later and the Delphi developers have had the benefit of seeing how another company had tackled the same problem.

Compilers and Interpreters

One of the main reasons for switching from Visual Basic to Delphi is that Delphi programs run much faster. A speed improvement of 10 times is not uncommon. This is largely due to Visual Basic interpreting your program code while Delphi is a full blown compiler. When you produce an application in Visual Basic, you need to distribute a DLL file called VBRUN40032.DLL with your program. This DLL file is about 400 Kbytes in size and so, although Visual Basic programs tend to be smaller than Delphi programs, when the size of the DLL is added, Delphi programs may win on size. The smallest Delphi program that you can generate is about 200 Kbytes.

The down side of using a compiled system rather than an interpreted one is the need to compile and link your program every time after making any changes. Fortunately, Delphi has a fast compiler but, if you have a very large application, Delphi may take minutes to compile and link all components of the system. However, many large applications written in Delphi would not be viable in Visual Basic since they would run too slowly.

Declaring Variables

In Delphi, before you use any variables you have to declare what type they are. In Visual Basic you have the option of doing this; in fact, you can set a configuration option so that all variables must be declared before being used. Good Visual Basic programmers use this option. If it is not used and a variable is mispelt, Visual Basic simply thinks that a new variable is being implicitly declared and does not flag an error. Debugging programs is hard enough without having to deal with this type of problem.

Type Checking

When you are assigning variables to each other when you do arithmetic or manipulate strings, Delphi checks to see that the variables that you are using are of the same type. In Visual Basic there is a strange data type called **Variant** which takes on the type of the variable it is assigned to. This can lead to unexpected results. The data type has now been included in version 2.0 of Delphi, however it is regarded by many programmers as a retrograde step.

In Visual Basic there are two ways of specifying the types of variables: you can use a variable declaration statement or alternatively you can use a type specifier character when you first use the variable, for example, the variable **value%** is an integer; **value!** is a floating point number. This is a hangover from earlier versions of Basic, but it can be useful to make clear what variable type you are using. In addition to the usual data types, Delphi also supports the **Real** and the **Extended** floating point types.

Using Strings

One area where Visual Basic has the edge over Delphi is that string manipulation is very straightforward. In Visual Basic you can do useful things such as concatenate two or more strings. For example:

> *first_hobby$ = "alligator wrestling"*
> *second_hobby$ = "insulting bouncers"*
> **Print** *("My hobbies are ", first_hobby$," and ", second_hobby$)*

gives the message:

> *"My hobbies are wrestling alligators and insulting bouncers"*

In Delphi, strings are treated as a character count followed by the characters themselves.

High-Level File Commands

One very useful feature of Visual Basic that is not available in Delphi is that there is a number of high- level commands for manipulating files. For example:

> *Kill "temp.txt"*

deletes a file and

> *Filecopy "first.bmp" "second.bmp"*

copies the entire contents of one file to another.

Database Access

A major selling point of Visual Basic is that it contains the engine for the Access database system. Not only can you read and update existing databases, but you can also create new databases. Since Visual Basic and Access are so closely integrated, the two packages work extremely well together, which is a great advantage. However, if you want to use another database, Visual Basic has no advantage over Delphi. Delphi has the excellent **Database Form Expert**, which makes it much easier to build database applications.

Which is Better?

This question is a difficult one to answer; Visual Basic can be used for faster development since programs do not have to be compiled before being run, but it cannot be used for some applications since the fact that it is not compiled will slow down the execution speed.

The Visual Basic language has very good string manipulation, but Delphi has much stronger type checking and a wider range of variable types. Both Basic and Pascal have their good and bad points – it depends on which you prefer, but both of these languages are excellent implementations.

The user interfaces are very similar, but I find that the Delphi environment is more logically organised. Delphi was clearly developed with an eye to what the Visual Basic developers had created and improvements made.

Delphi specifies that a more powerful minimum platform is required than for Visual Basic; however, in reality both require at least a 486 with at least 8 Mb. Both are improved by a Pentium with 16 Mb.

Which is better? It depends on the type of applications that you want to develop and which language you prefer. I am pleased that Visual Basic now has a strong competitor in Delphi – it can only make both systems better.

Index